Country Classics

Ginger Mitchell & Patsy Tompkins

Published by

Country Classics
19750 Peyton Highway
Peyton, CO 80831
(303) 648-3934
or
(719) 590-7818

For ordering information write or call:

Country Classics
19750 Peyton Highway
Peyton, CO 80831
(303) 648-3934

or

Country Classics
423 Red Mountain Court
Colorado Springs, CO 80919
(719) 590-7818

ISBN 0-9646160-0-9
Copyright © 1995, Ginger Mitchell and Patsy Tompkins
First Printing, June, 1995
Second Printing, December, 1995

Printed in the USA by

WIMMER
The Wimmer Companies, Inc.
Memphis

Introduction

This collection of recipes is compiled from many years of cooking. Some of them are family favorites that have been passed down for several generations and some we have collected, altered and personalized to meet our needs.

We grew up in a large family on the plains in Southeastern Colorado. Mom taught us at an early age, how to "make our way around the kitchen" and we haven't stopped yet.

We were partners in The Rollin' Pin Bakery and Restaurant from the late 70's to the late 80's. Our customers were always asking for our recipes, and now we are delighted to share them.

These recipes are not fancy - just down home cookin'! Most of them call for ingredients you have in your pantry and do not take hours to prepare. They have all been enjoyed by our families, friends, guests and customers and we hope you enjoy them too!

Dedication

We dedicate this book to our husbands and children, Art, Matthew and Michelle Mitchell; Michael Tompkins, Janey Bevans, Tacy Killingsworth, Bret and Cody Wager. They have been the ones who sampled all the experiments, gave us suggestions, enjoyed all their favorites and always ask for more! We love and appreciate them for their support.

Acknowledgements

Our special thanks to both our artist and photographer for their work and cooperation in making our dream come true.

Photo by M & R Photography/Mark Riese
Mark Riese has been doing photography for 10 years. He has experience in various types of photography including portrait, glamour, auto racing, (pro and amateur) and outdoor scenes.

Art work by Gwen Fox
Gwen Fox is an experimental watermedia artist whose work has been selected to show with paintings by His Royal Highness Prince Philip, a painting selected for a California wine label, accepted into and received awards in many national and international shows. Her paintings are in private and corporate collections.

Table of Contents

Appetizers &
Beverages

Cheese Log

1 (8 ounce) package cream
    cheese
1 (7 ounce) jar pineapple
    cheese spread
1 (7 ounce) jar bleu cheese
    spread (can use ½ cup
    bleu cheese dressing)
1 cup ground nuts

Mix cheeses together and chill for 30 minutes. Shape into logs and chill again. Before serving, pat nuts all over logs. Serve with any kind of crackers at your next party, very easy and good.

Sausage Balls

1 pound hot bulk sausage,
    room temperature
1½ cups sharp Cheddar
    cheese, grated
3 cups biscuit baking mix

Mix cheese with sausage, stir in biscuit baking mix. Roll into balls and refrigerate for one day before cooking. Heat oven to 375° and bake on a cookie sheet for 15 to 20 minutes. These are a great appetizer. You can freeze these on a cookie sheet, store in ziploc bag and use as needed for drop in guests.

Spinach Dip

1 package Ranch dressing
2 cups sour cream
1 (10 ounce) package frozen
    chopped spinach, drained
¼ cup onion, chopped
¾ teaspoon basil
½ teaspoon oregano
½ cup water chestnuts,
    chopped

Cook spinach and drain, combine all ingredients. Stir to blend. Chill for at least 1 hour so flavors blend. Serve in a hollowed out round loaf of Sheppard's bread. Cube hollowed out portion of bread and serve along with crackers and veggies. This is always a favorite.

Deviled Clam Mushrooms

12 large mushrooms
Margarine, melted
1 clove garlic, minced
2 tablespoons flour
1 (6½ ounce) can minced
    clams, drained, reserving
    2 tablespoons liquid
1 cup fresh bread crumbs
    (2 slices)
1 tablespoon parsley,
    chopped
2 teaspoons Worcestershire
    sauce
½ teaspoon dry mustard

Remove and finely chop mushroom stems; set aside. Brush caps with melted margarine. In medium skillet, cook garlic in 1 tablespoon margarine until tender. Stir in flour. Add chopped mushroom stems and remaining ingredients except mushroom caps; mix well. Mound into mushroom caps; place in shallow baking pan. Bake at 400° for 8 to 10 minutes or until hot. Refrigerate leftovers. These are so yummy. Makes 12 appetizers

Potato Sticks

3 medium baking potatoes
    (about 1 pound)
3 tablespoons Parmesan
    cheese
2 tablespoons chopped fresh
    oregano or 2 teaspoons
    dried oregano
2 teaspoons paprika
1 teaspoon garlic powder

Microwave directions: Scrub potatoes; cut each into 8 lengthwise spears. Spray potato spears with cooking spray. In plastic bag, combine cheese, oregano, paprika and garlic powder. Add potatoes; shake to coat. Spray 12 x 8-inch (2 quart) microwave-safe dish with cooking spray. Arrange potatoes in dish. Microwave on HIGH for 8 to 12 minutes or until tender, rotating dish once halfway through cooking. These are great dipped in salsa and sour cream. Serves 3

Crunchy Trail Mix

4 cups crispy corn cereal
  squares
1 cup peanuts
1 cup raisins
½ cup dried apples, cut into
  pieces
1 (12 ounce) package plain
  chocolate pieces

In large bowl, combine all ingredients; mix well. Store in loosely covered container. Great snack for kids when they get home from school. Makes 8½ cups

Goblin Goodies

2 cups salted peanuts
  (can use dry roasted)
1 cup chocolate Teddy
  grahams
1 cup candy corn
½ cup goldfish crackers
½ cup raisins

In large bowl, combine all ingredients. Store in covered container. Great Halloween treats. Makes 5 cups

Traditional Party Mix

¼ cup margarine
1¼ teaspoons seasoned salt
4½ teaspoons
  Worcestershire sauce
8 cups of your favorite Chex
  brand cereals (Corn, Rice
  and/or Wheat)
1 cup salted mixed nuts
1 cup pretzel sticks

Melt margarine in open roasting pan in preheated 250° oven. Stir in seasonings. Add cereals, nuts and pretzels; stir to coat evenly. Bake 1 hour, stirring every 15 minutes. Spread on absorbent paper to cool. Store in airtight container. Excellent snacks for after school and parties.

Creamy Hot Crab Dip

1 (8 ounce) package cream cheese, softened
1 tablespoon dry white wine
2 tablespoons onion, chopped
½ teaspoon prepared white horseradish
¼ teaspoon salt
⅛ teaspoon pepper
½ pound crabmeat
¼ cup almonds, sliced

In medium bowl, combine cream cheese and wine. Blend well. Mix in onion, horseradish, salt and pepper. Fold in crabmeat. Transfer mixture to a small shallow baking dish and sprinkle almonds over top. Bake at 375° for 15 minutes, or until almonds are golden brown and mixture is hot and bubbly. Remove from oven and serve with crackers. Yummy!

Chicken Wings

24-30 chicken wings
1 cup soy sauce
1 cup water
¾ cup sugar
¼ cup salad oil
1 tablespoon ginger
1 tablespoon garlic powder
½ cup pineapple juice

Combine all ingredients. Place in oven-proof glass baking dish and cover. Marinate overnight in refrigerator. Bake at 350° for one hour. Serves 6

Spicy Dip

2 cups pinto beans
1 cup sour cream
¼ cup green onion, sliced
¼ cup green chilies, diced
½ teaspoon garlic salt
1 teaspoon Worcestershire sauce
3 drops Tabasco sauce

Puree pinto beans. Add all other ingredients, mix well. Serve as a dip with corn or tortilla chips. Top this with a layer of guacamole and grated cheese for a wonderful variation. Makes about 3 cups

Chili Cheese Log

1 package chili seasoning
2 (8 ounce) packages cream
   cheese
3 tablespoons salsa
Chopped nuts

Beat all together. Shape into ball and top with chopped nuts. Chill until firm. Garnish with parsley or cilantro. Serve with assorted crackers and vegetables.

Spinach Balls

2 (10 ounce) packages
   chopped spinach, cooked
   and drained
2 cups stuffing mix
1 cup Parmesan cheese
¾ cup margarine, melted

Mix all ingredients together. Roll into balls and bake in preheated 350° oven for 20 - 25 minutes. The cheese and spinach makes these such a tasty treat. Makes 5 dozen

Bacon Filled Cherry Tomatoes

1 pound bacon, fried and
   crumbled
¼ cup green onions, chopped
2 tablespoons parsley,
   chopped
½ cup mayonnaise
24 cherry tomatoes

Combine ingredients except tomatoes. Cut a thin slice off top of each tomato. With a small spoon or melon baller, hollow out tomato. Fill tomatoes with bacon mixture. Make these when you are alone because your family will eat them faster than you can put them together! These were always a favorite when we catered parties. Makes 24

Vegetable Pizza

2 packages crescent rolls
2 (8 ounce) packages cream
    cheese
1 package Ranch dressing
1 cup mayonnaise
¾ cup green onions, chopped
¾ cup green pepper,
    chopped
¾ cup carrots, grated
¾ cup cauliflower, chopped
¾ cup broccoli, chopped
¾ cup ripe olives, sliced
¾ cup Cheddar cheese,
    grated

Place crescent rolls flat on a 15½ x 10½ cookie sheet, pinching seams together, forming a crust. Bake according to directions on crescent rolls. Cool. Mix cream cheese, Ranch dressing and mayonnaise. Spread mixture over crust. Layer vegetables on top. Cover with waxed paper and gently press vegetables into cream cheese. Refrigerate overnight or several hours. When ready to serve, remove waxed paper, and sprinkle cheese on top of pizza. Cut into small squares. You can use fresh vegetables of your choice. This is so good and everyone loves them.

Mexican Egg Rolls

½ pound ground beef
½ cup onion, chopped
1 clove garlic, minced
½ teaspoon cumin
½ teaspoon chili powder
¼ teaspoon salt
1 package egg roll wraps
1 egg yolk, beaten
1 package alfalfa sprouts
Oil

Brown beef with onions and garlic. Add seasonings. Drain if necessary. Take an egg roll wrap, put 1 to 2 tablespoons of meat mixture in the center, top with a tablespoon of alfalfa sprouts. Have a corner of the egg roll facing you. Fold corner to the center, fold each side corner to the center and roll away from you to form egg roll. Brush last corner with egg yolk to seal the roll. Deep fry in oil until golden brown. Drain and serve with guacamole. These are super!

Pico De Gallo

2 small tomatoes, chopped
4 green onions, sliced
⅔ cup cucumber, chopped
6 radishes, chopped
½ cup cilantro, chopped
2 or 3 serrano peppers,
    seeded and chopped
Juice of ½ lime
½ teaspoon garlic salt

Mix together and serve with chips or on your beef and chicken fajitas. This is excellent!

Texas Bean Dip

1 (16 ounce) can refried
    beans
1 (4 ounce) can green chilies
1 (3 ounce) package cream
    cheese
1 (4½ ounce) can ripe olives,
    chopped
1 to 2 teaspoons chili powder
⅓ cup sour cream
¾ cup Cheddar cheese,
    grated

In small baking dish, combine beans, cream cheese, olives, chili powder and sour cream. Top with grated cheese. Bake at 350° for 15-20 minutes or until bubbly. Serve with tortilla or corn chips. This is a wonderful dip, usually the first dish to be empty at a party. Makes 4 cups

Cheesy Salsa Dip

1 cup salsa
4 ounces cream cheese
1 cup Monterey Jack cheese,
    grated
2 tablespoons green onions,
    sliced

Microwave Directions: In medium microwave-safe bowl, combine salsa and cheeses. Microwave on HIGH for 2 to 4 minutes or until cheese is melted, stirring twice during cooking. Sprinkle with onions. Serve immediately with tortilla chips.

Tortilla Pinwheels

Filling
1 cup sour cream
1 (8 ounce) package cream
   cheese, softened
1 (4 ounce) can green chilies,
   diced
1 (4 ounce) can black olives,
   chopped and drained
1 cup Cheddar cheese,
   grated
½ cup green onion, chopped
Garlic powder to taste
Seasoned salt to taste

5 (10 inch) flour tortillas
Fresh parsley for garnish
Salsa

Mix all filling ingredients together. Divide filling and spread evenly over tortillas; roll up tortillas. Cover tightly with plastic wrap, twisting ends; refrigerate for several hours. Unwrap; cut in ½ inch slices. Discard ends. Lay pinwheels flat on glass serving plate; garnish with parsley. Leave space in center of plate for small bowl of salsa, if desired. Makes 3 to 4 dozen

Italian Crackers

Nonstick cooking spray
1 (10 ounce) package oyster
   crackers
1 teaspoon dried Italian
   seasoning
¼ teaspoon garlic powder
1 tablespoon Parmesan
   cheese

Spray cookie sheet with cooking spray. Spread crackers on cookie sheet. Spray crackers with cooking spray. Sprinkle with Italian seasoning and garlic powder; toss to coat. Bake at 325° for 10 to 15 minutes, stirring once. Sprinkle with cheese. Cool completely. Store in ziploc bag. These are a good snack and great croutons for salads and soups. Makes 6 cups

Wassail

1 gallon apple cider
1 (16 ounce) can frozen
   orange juice, undiluted
1 (12 ounce) can frozen
   lemonade, undiluted
2 cups rum (optional)
7 cinnamon sticks
¼ cup whole cloves

Simmer and serve hot. This is wonderful for holidays or any cold winter night.

Mulled Apple Cider

2 quarts apple cider
⅔ cup brown sugar
¼ teaspoon salt
6 whole cloves
6 whole allspice
4 cinnamon sticks
1 orange, sliced
1 apple, sliced

Mix in large kettle. Simmer. Serve either hot or cold. Not only is this delicious, but it makes your house smell great. I have made this in a 20 or 30 cup coffee pot and put spices and fruit in coffee basket - it works great!

Learn to be a good listener.

Wine Punch

1 (12 ounce) package frozen
  strawberries, thawed
2 lemons sliced
2 limes, sliced
1 cup grenadine
2 bottles white wine
1 (2 liter) Squirt or 7-Up

Mash strawberries, lemons and limes in punch bowl. Pour in other ingredients. This punch is so pretty and very tasty.

Easy Punch

1 (46 ounce) can pineapple
  juice
1 (46 ounce) can orange juice
1 quart cranberry juice
6 lemons, juiced
2 cups hot water
Sugar to taste
1 (6 ounce) package
  strawberry Jello
2 quarts ginger ale

Dissolve Jello in hot water, add all ingredients except ginger ale and stir. Add ginger ale just before serving. Put in punch bowl, add a pretty ice ring and serve at your party.

Goals should identify minimum performance. They should never limit your performance.

Fresh Cranberry Punch

4 cups fresh cranberries
3½ quarts water
12 whole cloves
4 cinnamon sticks
¾ cup orange juice
⅔ cup fresh lemon juice
2 cups sugar

Combine berries, water, cloves and cinnamon. Boil and simmer 15 minutes, covered. Strain juice through sieve or cheese cloth. Add orange juice, lemon juice and sugar. Stir until sugar is dissolved. Serve hot.

Champagne Punch

1 (16 ounce) can frozen
   lemonade, undiluted
1 (46 ounce) can pineapple
   juice (unsweetened)
1 bottle wine
2 bottles champagne
1 (10 ounce) box frozen
   strawberries, juice and all

Put in punch bowl, add ice mold and enjoy. It does not matter what wine or champagne you use - whatever is on sale. Excellent!

A smile is a curve that sets things straight.

Lulu's Punch

9 cups water
1½ cups sugar
1 (12 ounce) can frozen
   orange juice, undiluted
1 (12 ounce) can frozen
   lemonade, undiluted
1 quart vodka

Boil first two ingredients, dissolving sugar. Add orange juice, lemonade and vodka. Mix together and freeze.

To serve, fill glass half full with frozen mixture and add Sprite or 7-Up to fill the glass. This is yummy!!

Sherbet Punch

1 (12 ounce) can frozen pink
   lemonade, undiluted
1 (2 quart) container
   raspberry sherbet
2 (2 liter) bottles Sprite

Mix together in punch bowl. Makes a pretty and refreshing punch. Kids love this punch!

Failure only comes with quitting.

Best Ever Margaritas

3 shots tequila
1 shot triple sec
1 (6 ounce) can limeade,
    undiluted
1 (12 ounce) can grapefruit
    soda
15 - 20 ice cubes
Coarse salt
Lime

Pour tequila, triple sec, limeade and soda into blender. Add ice and continue blending until slushy. Rub rims of glasses with a slice of fresh lime and dip in coarse salt. Pour margaritas into prepared glasses. Enjoy!

Instant Cocoa

1 (8 quart) box powder milk
3½ cups powdered sugar
1 large jar creamer
1 large can instant chocolate

Mix and store in airtight container. To serve, use three tablespoons of mix per cup of hot water. Wonderful for kids after playing in the snow.

Brunch

Crunchy French Toast

3 eggs
1 cup milk
2 tablespoons sugar
1 teaspoon vanilla
½ teaspoon salt
3 cups cornflakes cereal,
   crushed to 1 cup
8 diagonally-cut slices
   French bread (¾ inch
   thick)
Strawberry syrup
Fresh strawberries

In shallow bowl, combine eggs, milk, sugar, vanilla and salt; mix well. Place crushed cereal in shallow bowl. Dip bread in egg mixture, making sure all egg mixture is absorbed. Dip bread into crumbs. Place in greased pan; cover. Freeze 1 to 2 hours or until firm. Heat oven to 425°. Bake 15 to 20 minutes or until golden brown, turning once. Serve with syrup. Garnish with strawberries and whipped topping if desired. This is very good and a different twist with the cereal coating. Serves 4

Walnut French Toast

8 thick slices soft French
   bread
8 eggs
1 teaspoon vanilla
½ cup milk
Pinch salt
½ cup walnuts, finely
   chopped
¾ cup sugar
1 teaspoon cinnamon
Warmed maple syrup for
   topping

Beat eggs with vanilla, milk and salt. Soak bread in eggs to coat both sides, turning once. Mix walnuts, sugar, and cinnamon in bowl; roll each bread slice in nut-sugar mixture to coat. Melt margarine in large sauté pan over medium heat. Sauté slices until golden brown and crispy on both sides, turning once. Serve with butter and warmed maple syrup. Serves 8

Oven-Puffed Berry Pancake

¼ cup margarine
3 large eggs
1 (3 ounce) package cream
   cheese
¾ cup milk
¾ cup flour
1½ cups sliced strawberries
½ cup each blueberries and
   raspberries
1 tablespoon powdered sugar
1 cup vanilla yogurt

Place margarine in a shallow 2 to 3 quart baking pan or dish. Set baking pan in 425° oven just until margarine melts, about five minutes. Meanwhile, put eggs, cream cheese, milk and flour in a food processor or blender; whirl until smoothly blended. Remove baking pan from oven and pour batter into pan. Return pan to oven and bake until batter puffs high and edges of the pancake are brown, about 25 to 30 minutes. Mix strawberries with blueberries and raspberries in a bowl. When pancake is done, remove from oven. To serve hot, fill with berries and dust with powdered sugar. To serve cool, set pancake aside up to 1 hour, then fill with fruit and dust with powdered sugar. Cut into wedges and serve with yogurt. This is delicious when berries are at their peak in summer. Serves 4 to 6

Mom's Pancakes

2 cups buttermilk
4 eggs, separated
4 tablespoons oil
2 cups flour
1 teaspoon soda
2 tablespoons sugar
4 teaspoons baking powder
1 teaspoon salt

Beat egg whites until very stiff. Set aside. Mix buttermilk and egg yolks. Add oil and dry ingredients. Fold in egg whites. Pour onto a hot griddle or skillet; cook until golden brown on each side. Serve with Dutch Honey (refer to index), maple syrup or fresh fruit. Serves 6

Apples and Cream Pancake

½ cup milk
2 eggs
½ cup flour
¼ teaspoon salt
1 to 2 tablespoons margarine
¼ cup brown sugar
1 (3 ounce) package cream
   cheese, softened
½ cup sour cream or yogurt
½ teaspoon vanilla
1½ cups apples, unpeeled
   and thinly sliced
¼ cup walnuts, chopped

In a small mixing bowl, combine milk, eggs, flour and salt. Beat until smooth. Heat a cast-iron or oven-proof skillet in a 450° oven until hot. Add margarine to the skillet; spread over entire bottom. Pour in batter; bake for 10 minutes or until golden brown. Meanwhile, combine sugar and cream cheese. Blend in sour cream or yogurt and vanilla. Fill pancake with ¾ cup cream cheese mixture and top with apples. Spread remaining cream cheese mixture over apples and sprinkle with nuts. Cut into wedges and serve immediately. This is a yummy brunch dish. Serves 4 to 6

Belgian Waffles

½ cup warm water
1 package yeast (2½
   teaspoons)
2 cups lukewarm milk
½ cup margarine, melted
1 teaspoon salt
1 tablespoon sugar
2 cups flour
2 eggs, beaten
1 teaspoon vanilla
Pinch soda

The night before you want to serve waffles, stir together in large bowl water and yeast. Allow to stand 10 minutes, stir in milk, margarine, salt and sugar. Beat in flour. Wrap bowl tightly with plastic wrap and let stand overnight on counter top - do not refrigerate. Next morning, preheat well-greased waffle iron. Stir in eggs, vanilla and soda. Beat well. Bake on prepared waffle iron until golden brown. Top with sliced fruit or use warm syrup. Serves 6

Dutch Honey

1 cup whipping cream
1 cup sugar
1 cup corn syrup (light or
   dark)

Mix in a saucepan and heat on low temperature until syrup is warm and sugar is dissolved. Serve warm. Refrigerate any leftover syrup. Can be reheated in microwave on low temperature. *This is another recipe that has been in our family for many years. We remember this at Grandma's house.*

Wonderful Granola

2½ cups regular oats
½ cup sunflower seeds
½ cup whole almonds
¼ cup bran (or wheat germ)
⅓ cup honey
½ cup brown sugar
⅓ cup margarine
1 teaspoon vanilla
½ teaspoon cinnamon
⅓ cup golden raisins, or
   other dried fruits

Combine in a small saucepan; margarine, brown sugar, honey and vanilla. Heat over low heat until sugar dissolves. Stir in bran or wheat germ. In large mixing bowl, combine everything else except dried fruit. Pour melted mixture over oat mixture and stir until coated well. Pour mixture into a 9 x 13 baking pan. Cook in a preheated 325° oven for 20-25 minutes stirring occasionally. Granola should be lightly toasted. Cool completely in a large mixing bowl, stirring often. Add dried fruits of your choice. Store in ziploc or airtight container. *This is great with yogurt or served with milk as a cereal.*

Excellence is achieved only through constant pursuit.

Phyllo Sausage Egg Bake

1 tablespoon margarine
1 medium onion, chopped
1 medium red bell pepper,
    chopped
1½ cups fresh mushrooms,
    sliced
½ pound bulk Italian sausage
5 eggs
1 cup Monterey Jack cheese,
    grated
1 (9 ounce) package frozen
    broccoli
1 cup ricotta cheese
1 tablespoon dried parsley
    flakes
20 phyllo pastry sheets
¾-1 cup margarine, melted

Melt 1 tablespoon margarine in skillet. Sauté peppers, onions, and mushrooms. Remove from skillet. In same skillet, brown sausage and drain. Add mushroom mixture to sausage. Beat eggs slightly, stir in cheese and mushroom-sausage mixture. In another bowl, combine broccoli, ricotta cheese and parsley. Unroll phyllo sheets and cover with plastic wrap. Place one sheet in ungreased 9 x 13 pan - fold to fit. Brush with melted margarine. Layer 4 more sheets, brushing each with margarine. Spread ½ sausage and mushroom mixture over phyllo. Layer and brush 5 more sheets. Spread with all broccoli mixture. Layer and brush 5 more sheets of phyllo. Spread last ½ of sausage and mushroom mixture. Layer and brush 5 more sheets of phyllo. Score top with diamond shapes. Bake at 350° for 50-60 minutes. Can make ahead. Cover and refrigerate for 2 to 24 hours. *This is a great brunch dish. Served with salad, it makes a hearty dinner.* Serves 8

True confidence is based on the thoroughness of preparation.

Asparagus and Crab Strata

12 slices white bread
½ cup margarine, softened
2 cups Cheddar cheese, grated
1 (9 ounce) package asparagus cuts, thawed and drained
6 ounces cooked crab or imitation crab, flaked
2½ cups milk
8 eggs
3 tablespoons parsley, chopped
1 teaspoon salt
1 teaspoon paprika
¼ teaspoon pepper

Spread margarine on one side of each slice of bread. Arrange six slices, margarine side down in 9 x 13 greased pan. Layer cheese, asparagus and crab over bread. Place remaining bread slices, margarine side up, over crab. In bowl, combine eggs, milk and seasonings. Pour over bread; let stand 10 to 15 minutes. Bake at 325° for 55 to 65 minutes or until knife inserted in center comes out clean. Can make ahead and refrigerate overnight. Serve with fresh fruit. *This is such a good brunch dish and when sliced, makes a pretty presentation.* Serves 8

Breakfast Casserole

1 pound bulk sausage, browned and drained
1¼ cups milk
7 slices bread, torn into pieces
1 cup Cheddar cheese, grated
1 teaspoon dry mustard
½ teaspoon salt
8 eggs

Layer bread, sausage and cheese in 9 x 13 inch pan. In blender, mix milk, eggs and mustard. Pour over bread and let stand at least 1 hour or can refrigerate overnight. Bake at 350° for 35 minutes. You can add mushrooms, onions, peppers, etc. to your casserole - whatever your family likes. *This is another great recipe that can be made ahead of time and adjusted to your family's liking.* Serves 8

Mexican Egg Bake

6 corn tortillas
12 eggs
½ cup milk
1 cup Cheddar cheese,
    grated
1 cup Monterey Jack cheese,
    grated
½ cup red bell pepper,
    chopped
1 (4 ounce) can diced green
    chilies

Sauce
1 tablespoon oil
1¼ cups fresh mushrooms,
    sliced
½ medium green bell pepper,
    chopped
1 (10 ounce) can mild
    enchilada sauce

Arrange tortillas in bottom of a 9 x 13 greased pan, overlapping edges. In large bowl, beat eggs and milk until well blended. Stir in cheeses, red pepper and chilies. Pour egg mixture over tortillas. Bake at 350° for 25 to 35 minutes or until knife inserted in center comes out clean. Meanwhile, heat oil in small saucepan over medium heat. Add mushrooms and green peppers; cook and stir until tender. Add enchilada sauce; heat thoroughly. Serve over baked egg mixture. This is a great dish with or without the sauce. Serves 8

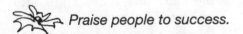

Praise people to success.

Chiliquilles

10-12 corn tortillas, cut into strips ½ inch wide and 2 inches long
1 onion, chopped
4 tablespoons margarine
1 dozen eggs, beaten
½ cup milk
½ teaspoon garlic salt
¼ teaspoon chili powder
¼ teaspoon cumin
Salt and pepper to taste
1 (4 ounce) can green chilies (fresh roasted chilies are wonderful)
1 cup Cheddar cheese, grated (can use half Monterey Jack)
1 tomato, peeled and chopped

Sauté tortilla strips and onion in margarine until softened. Beat eggs, add milk and seasonings. Pour over tortilla mixture. Cook, stirring until soft scrambled. Add green chilies, cheese and tomato. Stir until cheese melts. Serve with hash browns and toast for a hearty country breakfast. *This is a breakfast favorite when I cook for hunters in the fall.* Serves 8

Fried Apples

6 medium tart apples, unpeeled and sliced (Jonathan apples are best)
¼ cup margarine
½ cup sugar
1 teaspoon cinnamon
¼ cup water (more if needed)

In a skillet, heat margarine, add apples, sugar, cinnamon, and water. Cover. Simmer for about 20 minutes or until apples are tender. (If apple mixture starts to thicken before apples are tender, add a little more water.) *Our Mom used to serve these with fried quail, biscuits and gravy for breakfast when we were kids. They are also excellent served with pork.*

Fresh Apple Fritters

1 cup flour
2 tablespoons sugar
1 teaspoon baking powder
Dash salt
2 eggs, beaten
⅔ cup milk
1 teaspoon cooking oil
4 to 6 tart cooking apples,
    peeled, cored and sliced
    crosswise
Oil for frying
Granulated sugar

Stir together flour, sugar, baking powder and salt. Combine eggs, milk and 1 teaspoon cooking oil. Add to dry mixture; beat smooth. Dip apple slices, one at a time in batter to coat. Fry in shallow hot oil (375°) for about 2½ to 3 minutes or until brown and edges are crispy, turning once. Drain on paper towel. Sprinkle with granulated sugar. Makes 1½ to 2 dozen

Build a feeling of importance in every person you meet.

Soups & Sandwiches

Rollin' Pin Chowder

3 cups dried lima beans
7 cups water
1 cup celery, chopped
1½ cups carrots, chopped
1 medium onion, chopped
3 cups cabbage, shredded
¾ pound little smokie
   sausages
1 (15 ounce) can stewed
   tomatoes
1 cup uncooked pasta
   (macaroni or spirals)
1 teaspoon salt
½ teaspoon pepper
4 cups chicken broth

Cook lima beans until done. Add all ingredients except pasta and simmer until vegetables are crisp-tender. Add pasta and cook until done. Serve with French bread. *This was a popular soup from the Bakery.* Serves 8

Chicken Noodle Soup

1 whole chicken (2 to 3
   pounds)
2½ quarts water
3 teaspoons salt
2 chicken bouillon cubes
½ medium onion, chopped
⅛ teaspoon pepper
¼ teaspoon dried marjoram
¼ teaspoon dried thyme
1 bay leaf
1 cup carrots, sliced
1 cup celery, sliced
1½ cups uncooked fine
   noodles

In large soup kettle, place chicken and all ingredients except noodles. Cover and bring to a boil; skim broth. Reduce heat; cover and simmer 1½ hours or until chicken is tender. Remove chicken from broth; allow to cool. Debone chicken and cut into chunks. Skim fat from broth; bring to a boil. Add noodles; cook until noodles are done. Return chicken to kettle; adjust seasonings to taste. Remove bay leaf before serving. *And who doesn't like chicken noodle soup!* Serves 8

Taco Soup

2 pounds ground beef
1 onion, chopped
1 (7 ounce) can green chilies,
    diced
1 teaspoon salt
1 teaspoon pepper
1 (15 ounce) can pinto beans,
    drained
1 (15 ounce) can lima beans,
    drained
1 (15 ounce) can hominy,
    drained
1 (15 ounce) can kidney
    beans, drained
1 package taco seasoning
1 package Ranch dressing
1 (16 ounce) can stewed
    tomatoes
1 quart tomato juice

Brown beef and onions, drain. Add all remaining ingredients. Bring to boil and simmer 30 minutes. Top with Cheddar cheese. *Excellent quick meal - this is something you can put together after a long day at work. Serve with warm tortillas or cornbread.* Serves 8

Chicken and Rice Soup

10 cups chicken broth
1 medium onion, chopped
1 cup celery, sliced
1 cup carrots, sliced
¼ cup parsley, chopped
½ teaspoon pepper
½ teaspoon thyme
1 bay leaf
1½ cups cooked chicken,
    cubed
2 cups cooked rice
2 tablespoons fresh lemon
    juice

Combine broth, onions, celery, carrots, parsley, pepper, thyme, and bay leaf in Dutch oven. Bring to a boil. Reduce heat; simmer, uncovered, 10 to 15 minutes. Add chicken; simmer uncovered, 5 to 10 minutes. Remove and discard bay leaf. Stir in rice and lemon juice just before serving. *Served with salad and French bread, makes a wonderful meal.* Serves 8

Hamburger Soup

1 pound ground beef
2 teaspoons beef-flavor
    instant bouillon
2 cups water
¼ teaspoon pepper
½ teaspoon salt
1 cup carrots, sliced
1 cup celery, sliced
½ cup onion, chopped
2 (14 ounce) cans stewed
    tomatoes

Boil hamburger in water until it is brown (until meat is not pink). Add all other ingredients and simmer until vegetables are tender. *Excellent meal on a cold evening. (You can add macaroni for variation and to make it go further.)* Serves 8

Cheese Soup

1½ cups carrots, chopped
1 cup celery, chopped
1 medium onion, chopped
2 cups milk
⅓ cup margarine
1 (14½ ounce) can chicken
    broth
1 tablespoon dried parsley
6 tablespoons flour
¼ pound Cheddar cheese,
    grated

Chop carrots, celery and onions together. Put in microwave. Cook until tender. Add 1 can chicken broth and parsley to hot vegetables. Stir and set aside. Heat together ⅓ cup margarine and 6 tablespoons flour as thickener. Add at least 2 cups milk. Cook and stir until thickened. (You can use ¼ pound or more if you like it really cheesy.) Stir cheese into milk mixture, cook in microwave (take in and out, stirring every 1½ minutes). When mixture is hot, melted and smooth, add to very hot vegetables. (If vegetables have cooled, reheat before adding cheese). Serve with crusty French bread and enjoy. Makes 6 servings

Onion Soup

4 tablespoons unsalted
   butter
4 large sweet onions, sliced
1 tablespoon sugar
6 cups beef broth, divided
2 tablespoons
   Worcestershire sauce
¼ teaspoon pepper
½ teaspoon salt
4 thick slices French bread
Additional butter
Garlic salt
1 cup Swiss cheese, grated

In heavy pan, melt butter over medium heat. Sauté onions until tender. Sprinkle sugar over onions. Reduce heat and cook, stirring occasionally, until onions are caramelized. (About 20 minutes.) Add 3 cups broth; simmer 15 minutes. Add remaining broth, Worcestershire sauce, salt and pepper. Cover and simmer for 30-40 minutes. Meanwhile, spread both sides of bread with additional butter; sprinkle with garlic salt. Broil bread until golden brown on both sides. Ladle soup into individual oven-proof soup bowls. Float a slice of bread in each bowl and sprinkle with cheese. Broil until cheese is melted and bubbly. Serve immediately. *Soooo Good!* Serves 4

Split Pea Soup

1 (16 ounce) package split
   green peas
7 cups water
2 cups potatoes, diced
1 cup celery, sliced
1 (1½ pound) ham hock
1½ cups onions, chopped
1 cup carrots, sliced
1 teaspoon salt
1 clove garlic, minced
¼ teaspoon pepper

Rinse split peas under cold running water; drain. In large bowl, combine all ingredients. (May be prepared in advance to this point. Cover and refrigerate overnight.) Place in slow cooker. Cook on proper setting according to manufacturer's directions for 6 to 8 hours. Just before serving, remove ham hock. Cut meat from bone and return to soup. This can also be made on stove top if you prefer. *It is such a good soup.* Serves 8

Sausage and Pasta Soup

1½ pounds sweet Italian
   sausage or smoked
   sausage
1 medium onion, chopped
1 medium green pepper, cut
   into strips
1 clove garlic, minced
1 (28 ounce) can tomatoes,
   chopped
1 to 1½ cups uncooked bow
   tie pasta
6 cups water
1 tablespoon sugar
1 tablespoon Worcestershire
   sauce
2 chicken bouillon cubes
1 teaspoon dried basil
1 teaspoon dried thyme
1 teaspoon salt

Slice sausage into 1 inch pieces. In Dutch oven, brown sausage over medium heat. Remove sausage and drain all but 2 tablespoons of drippings. Sauté onion, pepper and garlic until tender. Add sausage and all remaining ingredients. Simmer, uncovered, stirring occasionally until pasta is tender, about 15-20 minutes. *This is one of our favorites. Serve with French bread or cornbread for a hearty meal.* Serves 8

Sausage Soup

4½ cups water
5 medium potatoes, peeled
   and cubed
1 medium onion, chopped
1 clove garlic, minced
½ teaspoon salt
1 teaspoon dill weed
¼ teaspoon caraway seed
1 teaspoon sugar
¾ pound sausage, cut up
   (smoked or Kielbasa)
1 pound sauerkraut,
   undrained
1 cup sour cream
1 tablespoon flour

In Dutch oven, bring water, potatoes and salt to boil. Cook, covered, over medium heat until potatoes are tender. Add sausage, sauerkraut, onion, garlic, dill, caraway seed and sugar. Bring to boil. Meanwhile, combine sour cream and flour in a bowl. Gradually stir one cup hot soup into this mixture and return to pan. Heat thoroughly, but do not boil. Add salt and pepper to taste. Serve with cornbread or French bread. *If you like sauerkraut, you'll love this soup!* Serves 8

Gazpacho

1 (46 ounce) can tomato juice
2 cups vegetable juice
2 tablespoons red wine
    vinegar
1 clove garlic, minced
1 teaspoon salt
½ teaspoon pepper
8 - 10 drops hot pepper sauce
2 tablespoons olive oil
1 medium cucumber, finely
    chopped
1 medium green pepper,
    finely chopped
Green onions, sliced
Croutons

Mix all ingredients together. Chill several hours. Serve with a dollop of sour cream and croutons. *Refreshing summertime lunch.* Serves 6

Three Bean Chili

3 strips bacon, fried and
    crumbled
1½ pounds ground beef
1 (15 ounce) can kidney
    beans
1 (15 ounce) can pinto beans
2 (15 ounce) cans chili beans
1 (8 ounce) can tomato sauce
1 (15 ounce) can stewed
    tomatoes
2 (4 ounce) cans mushrooms,
    sliced
2 cups tomato juice
1 large onion, chopped
1 teaspoon seasoned salt
1 teaspoon pepper
3 teaspoons chili powder, or
    to taste
1 clove garlic, minced
1 tablespoon parsley

Brown ground beef and onions. Drain if necessary. Add all other ingredients except bacon. Simmer for 2 to 3 hours. Stir in bacon just before serving. *This is a good change from traditional chili.* Serves 6

Santa Fe Soup

3 (14½ ounce) cans chicken
    broth
1 cup chicken, cooked and
    cubed
1 (4 ounce) can green chiles,
    chopped
1 cup onions, chopped
1 cup tomatoes, chopped
1 teaspoon dried cilantro
    leaves
1 teaspoon chili powder
¾ teaspoon cumin
¼ teaspoon salt
¼ teaspoon pepper
¼ teaspoon hot red pepper
    sauce
1 (16 ounce) package frozen
    corn with red and green
    peppers
1 cup tortilla chips, crushed
    coarsely
1½ cups Monterey Jack
    cheese, grated
Tortilla chips

In large saucepan, combine chicken broth, chicken, green chiles, onions, tomatoes, cilantro, chili powder, cumin, salt, pepper and hot pepper sauce. Bring to a boil. Reduce heat; simmer uncovered 10 minutes. Stir in vegetables; simmer uncovered 15 to 20 minutes or until vegetables are crisp-tender, stirring occasionally. Stir in 1 cup crushed chips and cheese. Heat until thoroughly heated and cheese melts, stirring frequently. Garnish with additional chips. Serve immediately. Serves 4

If you think you can, you can.

Confetti Bean Soup Mix

1 (16 ounce) package black
   beans
1 (16 ounce) package great
   Northern beans
1 (16 ounce) package dry red
   kidney beans
1 (16 ounce) package pinto
   beans
1 (16 ounce) package green
   split peas

Seasoning bag
3 beef flavored bouillon
   cubes
3 tablespoons dried chives,
   chopped
1 teaspoon salt
1 teaspoon dried savory
½ teaspoon cumin
½ teaspoon coarse ground
   pepper
1 bay leaf

Cut 4 (6 inch) squares of plastic wrap. Place bouillon cubes, chives, salt, savory, cumin pepper and bay leaf in each square. Tie each seasoning bag with ribbon or string.

Divide the beans into four bags and add one seasoning bag to each. Include directions for cooking Confetti Bean Soup Mix with each bag. Tie with a pretty bow. Makes great Christmas gifts. Makes 4 bags

Confetti Bean Soup Cooking Directions
Sort through beans and discard all shriveled beans. Rinse beans. In 5 quart Dutch oven, over high heat, heat beans and 9 cups water to boiling; cook 3 minutes. Remove from heat; cover and let stand 1 hour. Drain and rinse beans. Return beans to Dutch oven; add contents of seasoning bag and 5 cups water. Over high heat, heat to boiling. Reduce heat to low; cover and simmer 1½ hours or until beans are tender, stirring occasionally. Add one (16 ounce) can stewed tomatoes and its liquid. Heat to boiling. Reduce heat to low and cook uncovered 15 minutes longer, stirring to break up tomatoes. Discard bay leaf. For extra flavor, cook beans with ham hock. It is also good served over cooked rice. Serves 8

Chicken Tortellini Soup

1 (9 ounce) package frozen
   broccoli, thawed
6 cups water
3 (11 ounce) cans condensed
   chicken broth
1 (11 ounce) can cream of
   chicken soup
2 cups cooked chicken,
   cubed
1 cup onions, chopped
1 cup carrots, sliced
½ cup wine (optional)
2 cloves garlic, minced
½ teaspoon basil
½ teaspoon oregano
1 (7 ounce) package dried
   cheese tortellini
Parmesan cheese

In large Dutch oven, combine water, chicken broth, soup, chicken, onions, carrots, wine, garlic, basil and oregano. Bring to boil, simmer until veggies are crisp-tender, add tortellini. Simmer, uncovered 20 minutes or until tortellini is almost done. Add broccoli. Simmer an additional 5 to 10 minutes or until broccoli is tender and tortellini is done. Serve with Parmesan cheese. (If you use fresh tortellini, add 10 minutes before serving the soup.) *This is one of my family's favorites - serve with French bread or cornbread.*
Serves 8

Cook's Tips

Garnish individual bowls of soup with any one or a combination of the following:

Croutons
Oyster crackers
Bean sprouts
Peanuts
Lemon slices
Celery stalks
Crackers

Bacon, fried and crumbled
Mushrooms, sliced
Parsley, chopped
Basil, chopped
Chives, chopped
Cucumber, sliced thin
Mint or watercress

Enthusiasm is the key to positive living.

Turkey Salad Sandwich

1½ cups celery, diced
3 cups turkey, cooked and
   diced
1 cup pecans or walnuts,
   chopped
½ cup mayonnaise or lowfat
   yogurt
⅛ teaspoon ginger
1 tablespoon lemon juice

Mix turkey, celery, and nuts in large bowl. Blend mayonnaise, ginger, and lemon juice in small bowl. Pour dressing over turkey mixture and toss. Chill. Make into sandwiches on your favorite bread. (Chicken can be used instead of turkey.) This salad is also great on a bed of lettuce with tomato wedges. *A great Aunt gave us this recipe. Enjoy.*

Onion-Italian Sausage Sandwich

2 tablespoons margarine
6 medium onions, peeled and
   sliced ¼ inch thick
6 sweet Italian sausages or
   brats
1 small green pepper,
   chopped
1 small red pepper, chopped
1½ tablespoons Italian
   seasonings
Dash of soy sauce

Melt margarine in large skillet; add onions and cook until lightly browned. Remove; set aside. Brown sausages lightly in skillet, turning frequently. Remove; set aside with onions. Add more margarine to skillet if necessary and lightly brown peppers. Add onions, sausages, Italian seasonings and soy sauce to skillet. Add water to 1-inch depth and simmer until sausages are done and water is cooked away. Serve on hoagie buns. These truly make a meal. Makes 6 servings

Rollin' Pin Roast Beef Sandwich

Roast beef, thinly sliced
Broth
Sweet cherry peppers, sliced
Swiss cheese, sliced
Mustard
Mayonnaise
Sandwich rolls, wheat or
   white

Place roast beef in microwave safe dish and add enough broth to cover bottom of dish. Cover and heat until thoroughly warmed. Slice rolls, add mustard and/or mayonnaise. Place desired amount of beef slices on roll, add peppers and cheese. *This makes the world's best roast beef sandwich.* It is a great way to use extra roast beef. Serve with salad for a great meal. *These were the most popular sandwiches in our restaurant. Of course, we served them on homemade rolls.*

Shredded BBQ Beef Sandwich

5 pound chuck roast
½ cup brown sugar
¼ cup vinegar
2 cups water
2¾ cups catsup
1 tablespoon dry mustard
1 large onion, chopped
1 to 2 garlic cloves, minced
Sesame buns

Combine beef, brown sugar, vinegar and water in 6-quart cast-iron or heavy oven-proof pan. Bake at 375° for 3 hours covered. Remove from oven; cool. Remove all fat and any bones. Shred beef; return to pan. Add mixture of catsup, mustard, onion and garlic; stir to blend. Reduce oven temperature to 300° and cook, covered, for up to 4 hours. Stir every half hour, adding more water/catsup to keep well moistened. Serve on buns. *This is soooo good!* Makes 12 - 14 servings

French Dip Sandwich

1 lean beef roast (3 to 4
   pounds)
½ cup soy sauce
1 beef bouillon cube
1 bay leaf
3 to 4 whole peppercorns
1 teaspoon crushed
   rosemary
1 teaspoon thyme
1 teaspoon garlic powder
Hard rolls or French bread

Remove and discard all visible fat from roast. Place in a slow cooker. Combine soy sauce, bouillon and spices; pour over roast. Add water to almost cover roast. Cover and cook over low heat 10-12 hours or until meat is very tender. Remove meat from broth; reserve broth. Shred meat with a fork. Serve on hard rolls or French bread. Serve with broth for dipping. Makes 12 sandwiches

Marinated Flank Steak Sandwich

⅔ cup beer
⅓ cup oil
½ teaspoon salt
¼ teaspoon garlic salt
¼ teaspoon pepper
2 tablespoons margarine
½ teaspoon paprika
1 to 2 onions, sliced
1 cup sour cream
1 teaspoon horseradish
2 pounds flank steak,
   about 1 inch thick

In shallow dish, combine beer, oil, salt, garlic salt and pepper. Place flank steak in marinade; cover. Marinate overnight in refrigerator or several hours at room temperature; drain. Grill steak 5 to 7 minutes on each side for medium rare. In a saucepan, melt margarine; blend in paprika and a dash of salt. Add onions, cook until tender, but not brown. Combine sour cream and horseradish, heat with onions. Thinly slice meat on diagonal, across grain, and top with sour cream and onion mixture. Serve on your favorite sandwich roll. These are wonderful sandwiches. Serves 4

Mandarin Chicken Pockets

1 cup cooked chicken, cubed
1 (11 ounce) can mandarin
   orange segments, drained
½ cup celery, chopped
¼ cup almonds, sliced
2 green onions, sliced
3 tablespoons mayonnaise
¼ teaspoon salt
Dash pepper
3 (6 inch) pitas, halved
1½ cups alfalfa sprouts

In medium bowl, combine all ingredients except pitas and alfalfa sprouts; mix well. Fill each pita half with ⅓ cup chicken mixture and ¼ cup sprouts. The oranges add a bit of sweetness to this chicken salad. You can make this ahead of time, refrigerate and assemble sandwiches when ready to serve. Serves 4

Breads

Nutty Rhubarb Muffins

¾ cup brown sugar
½ cup buttermilk
½ cup oil
1 egg
1 teaspoon vanilla
2 cups flour
½ teaspoon soda
½ teaspoon salt
1 cup rhubarb, diced
½ cup nuts, chopped

Topping
¼ cup brown sugar
½ cup nuts
½ teaspoon cinnamon

Mix together brown sugar, buttermilk, oil, egg and vanilla. Add dry ingredients. Stir in rhubarb and nuts. Put in greased or paper-lined muffin tin. Sprinkle with topping. Bake at 375° for 30 minutes or until golden brown. Makes 12

Blueberry Muffins

1¾ cups flour
½ cup sugar
1 teaspoon baking powder
¾ teaspoon salt
½ teaspoon soda
1 egg, well beaten
1 cup buttermilk
6 tablespoons margarine, melted
1½ teaspoons vanilla
1 cup blueberries, fresh or frozen

Mix dry ingredients together. Mix buttermilk, egg, margarine and vanilla together. Add to dry ingredients, stir just to moisten. Add blueberries and stir gently (do not over stir). Bake at 400° for 25 minutes in greased or paper-lined muffin tin. (Can be baked in loaf pan at 350° for 45 minutes.) These are excellent muffins. Makes 12

Obstacles either polish us up or wear us down.

Apple Muffins

1¾ cups flour
½ cup sugar
1 teaspoon cinnamon
1 teaspoon baking powder
¾ teaspoon salt
½ teaspoon soda
1 egg, well beaten
1 cup buttermilk
6 tablespoons margarine,
　melted
1 teaspoon vanilla
1 cup apples, peeled and
　chopped
½ cup nuts, chopped

Mix dry ingredients together. Mix buttermilk, egg, margarine and vanilla together. Add to dry ingredients, stir just to moisten. Stir in apples and nuts (do not over stir). Bake at 400° for 25 minutes in a greased or paper-lined tin. These are excellent with Jonathan apples in the fall. Makes 12

Pumpkin Chocolate Chip Muffins

½ cup almonds, sliced
1⅔ cups flour
1 cup sugar
1 teaspoon cinnamon
　(pumpkin pie spice is
　good)
1 teaspoon soda
¼ teaspoon baking powder
¼ teaspoon salt
2 eggs
1 cup pumpkin
½ cup margarine, melted
1 cup chocolate chips

Thoroughly mix dry ingredients together in large bowl. In medium bowl, add eggs, pumpkin and margarine. Whisk until well blended. Stir in chocolate chips and almonds. Pour over dry ingredients and fold in with rubber spatula, just until dry ingredients are moistened. Scoop batter into greased or paper-lined muffin tin. Bake at 350° for 20 to 25 minutes or until springs back when touched. Can be served with Cream Cheese Spread. (refer to page 143) Makes 12

Doris' Biscuits

2 cups flour
2 teaspoons sugar
1 teaspoon cream of tartar
1 teaspoon soda
3 teaspoons baking powder
1 teaspoon salt
1¼ cups cream

Mix dry ingredients. Add cream and stir just until moistened. Knead gently on floured board. Roll to 1 inch thickness and cut with biscuit cutter. Bake at 400° until golden brown.

Quick Dinner Rolls

2 tablespoons shortening
1 cup warm water
¼ cup sugar
½ teaspoon salt
¼ cup lukewarm water
1 teaspoon sugar
1 package yeast (2½ teaspoons)
4 cups flour
1 egg

Mix first four ingredients. Dissolve yeast in ¼ cup lukewarm water and 1 teaspoon sugar. Combine yeast mixture with first mixture, add egg and 2 cups flour, beat well, add remaining flour, stir until moistened. Knead until smooth, place in greased bowl. Let rise until double in bulk, about 1 hour. Make into 12 to 15 rolls. Grease a cookie sheet, place rolls side by side nearly touching. Cover with tea towel and let rise for 1 hour or until double. Bake at 425° for 15 to 20 minutes. This can also be made into a loaf and baked 30 to 35 minutes.

Plan your work and work your plan.

Yeast Buttermilk Biscuits

1 tablespoon sugar
2 tablespoons lukewarm
   water
1 package yeast (2½
   teaspoons)
2 cups flour
1 teaspoon baking powder
1 teaspoon salt
2 tablespoons shortening
⅔ cup buttermilk

In small bowl, mix sugar and water. Add yeast and stir to dissolve. Mix flour, baking powder and salt into large bowl. Cut in shortening to fine crumb stage. Add buttermilk and yeast mixture. Mix to moderately stiff dough. Knead lightly for a few seconds. Roll to ½ inch thickness, cut into biscuits. Place on greased cookie sheet, prick tops with fork and brush with melted margarine. Let rise in warm place until almost double. Bake at 425° for 12 to 18 minutes. Makes 12

Hot Cross Buns

4½ to 5 cups flour
½ cup sugar
½ teaspoon cinnamon
¼ teaspoon salt
1 package yeast (2½
   teaspoons)
1 cup milk
½ cup margarine
1 egg
1 cup raisins
1 egg yolk

Frosting
1 cup powdered sugar
1 tablespoon margarine
Enough warm water to make
   desired consistency

Combine 1 cup flour, sugar, cinnamon, salt and yeast. Heat milk, margarine and ¼ cup water until very warm. Add to flour mixture and beat 2 minutes. Beat in egg and 1 cup flour, continue beating. Stir in 2 cups flour (enough to make soft dough). Add raisins. Knead, let rise until double, about 2 hours. Punch down and put on floured surface, cover with towel for 15 minutes. Shape into rolls. Beat egg yolk with 2 teaspoons water. Brush rolls with mixture. Let rise until double - about 30 minutes. Make cross on buns with scissors and bake at 350° for 30 minutes. Serve warm. Frost just before serving.

Danish Pastry

2 packages yeast
   (5 teaspoons)
½ cup warm water
1 teaspoon sugar
¼ cup margarine
½ cup sugar
1 teaspoon salt
2 eggs
4 cups flour
1 cup warm milk
1½ cups margarine

Glaze
2 cups powdered sugar
Pinch of salt
½ teaspoon almond extract
1 tablespoon margarine
Hot water to make soft glaze

Sprinkle yeast into warm water and 1 teaspoon sugar. Set aside until yeast is activated and bubbles to top of cup. Beat margarine, sugar and salt. Add yeast, eggs and 1 cup flour. Beat well. Add 3 more cups flour alternately with 1 cup warm milk. Beat well after each addition. Cover with plate and set aside to rise for about an hour. Use a bowl with 1 gallon capacity and let rise until batter reaches plate. Pour dough on floured surface. Pat out to 12 x 18-inch oblong and put chips of cold margarine on ⅓ of surface. Fold over and put chips of margarine on remaining ⅓ and fold with margarine inside dough. Put chips of margarine on ⅓ of the folded dough and fold toward center. Put more margarine on the center ⅓ and fold the remaining dough over the margarine. Roll dough into 18 x 24-inch oblong. Cut into 4 strips which will be approximately 6 x 18-inch. Put your favorite filling in center of dough. Use fruit filling or Cream Cheese Filling (refer to page 143) or a combination of both. (You can use your favorite jam as filling.) Make 12 diagonal cuts on each side of filling. Pull ends of strips across filling, alternating from side to side, pressing down firmly each strip. This gives a

(Continued on next page)

(Danish Pastry, continued)

braided effect. Place on greased pan in circular shape and let rise for an hour or longer until double. Bake at 350° for 25 to 30 minutes until golden brown. Drizzle hot Danish with glaze. *These take a while to make, but are well worth it. This is the best Danish that we have ever eaten!*

Doughnuts

1 cup potatoes, mashed
½ cup sugar
1½ cups warm milk
2 teaspoons salt
⅓ cup shortening, melted
2 eggs
½ cup warm water
2 packages yeast (5
   teaspoons)
6 to 7 cups flour

Glaze
3 cups powdered sugar
1 teaspoon vanilla
1 tablespoon cornstarch
Warm water

Mix potatoes, sugar, milk, salt, shortening, eggs, water and yeast together. Add about 6 cups of flour until it is a thick consistency. Pour out on floured surface and knead for about five minutes until dough is smooth. Put back in greased bowl and let dough rise until double. Punch down and let rise again. Roll out to about ½ inch thickness, cut with doughnut cutter. Let doughnuts rise again until double. Fry in hot oil until golden brown. Drain on paper towels. Dip doughnuts in glaze or in sugar while warm. Mix the glaze together, add enough water to make a thin but not watery consistency. You can also add cocoa to glaze and have chocolate glazed doughnuts. *These doughnuts are fabulous! They were a favorite of our customers at the Rollin' Pin Bakery.*

Applesauce Cake Doughnuts

4 eggs
2 cups sugar
4 tablespoons oil
1½ cups buttermilk
2 cups applesauce
4 teaspoons baking powder
2 teaspoons soda
1 teaspoon salt
1 teaspoon cinnamon
½ teaspoon nutmeg
7 to 8 cups flour

Beat eggs, sugar and oil. Add buttermilk and applesauce. Stir in dry ingredients to make a thick dough. Chill dough several hours or overnight. Roll to ½ inch thickness on a lightly floured surface. Cut with doughnut cutter. Fry in hot oil until golden brown. Dip in glaze while hot. (Refer to glaze in Doughnut recipe.) A mixture of sugar and cinnamon is also good on this doughnut. *These are great doughnuts.*

Doughnut Drops

1¾ cups flour
¼ cup sugar
1 tablespoon baking powder
1 teaspoon salt
½ teaspoon nutmeg
¾ cup milk
1 egg
¼ cup oil

Mix dry ingredients. Beat egg, milk and oil together. Add to dry ingredients. Drop by teaspoons in 1 inch of hot oil. Fry until golden brown. Drain on paper towels. Shake in bag of 1 teaspoon nutmeg and 1 cup sugar. Makes about 4 dozen

 The person who is always willing to go the second mile will never come to a dead-end road.

Cinnamon Rolls

½ cup warm water
2 packages yeast (5
    teaspoons)
1½ cups warm milk
½ cup sugar
2 teaspoons salt
2 eggs
½ cup margarine, melted
7 to 7½ cups flour

Filling
1½ cups sugar
3 to 4 teaspoons cinnamon

Frosting
1½ cups powdered sugar
2 tablespoons margarine
1 teaspoon vanilla
Enough water to make
    spreading consistency

In large bowl, dissolve yeast in warm water. Add milk, sugar, salt, eggs, margarine and half of flour to yeast mixture. Mix until smooth. Add enough remaining flour to handle easily. Turn onto lightly floured surface; knead until smooth (about 5 minutes). Place in greased bowl; cover with towel. Let rise until double, punch down and let rise again until double. Punch down again and divide in half. Mix filling ingredients in small bowl. Roll dough into oblong shape on lightly floured surface. Brush with melted margarine and sprinkle desired amount of cinnamon and sugar mixture over margarine. Roll up tightly, beginning with wide edge. Cut into 1 inch slices. (Use a double piece of thread - slide under roll and cross over - pulling through roll. You won't squash the roll and lose filling like you do when slicing with a knife.) Place rolls on greased pan - do not place them too close together, they need room to rise up and out. Cover and let rise until double. Bake at 350° until golden brown. Frost while warm. *These were a favorite at the Rollin' Pin Bakery!*

Judge each day not by the harvest you reap but by the seeds you plant.

Strawberry Rhubarb Coffee Cake

Filling
3 cups fresh or frozen
   rhubarb, sliced
1 quart fresh strawberries,
   mashed
2 tablespoons lemon juice
1 cup sugar
⅓ cup cornstarch

Cake
3 cups flour
1 cup sugar
1 teaspoon baking powder
1 teaspoon soda
½ teaspoon salt
1 cup margarine, cut into
   pieces
1½ cups buttermilk
2 eggs
1 teaspoon vanilla

Topping
¼ cup margarine
¾ cup flour
¾ cup sugar

In large saucepan, combine rhubarb, strawberries and lemon juice. Cover and cook over medium heat about 5 minutes. Combine sugar and cornstarch; stir into saucepan. Bring to boil, stirring constantly until thickened; remove from heat and set aside. In large bowl, combine flour, sugar, baking powder, soda and salt. Cut in margarine until mixture resembles coarse crumbs. Beat buttermilk, eggs and vanilla; stir into crumb mixture. Spread half of batter evenly into greased 9 x 13 inch pan. Carefully spread filling on top. Drop remaining batter by spoonfuls over filling. For topping, melt margarine in saucepan over low heat. Remove from heat, stir in flour and sugar until mixture resembles coarse crumbs. Sprinkle over batter. Lay foil on lower rack to catch any juicy fruit spillovers. Place coffee cake on middle rack; bake at 350° for 40 to 45 minutes. Cool in pan, cut into squares. Serves 16

Peachy Sour Cream Coffee Cake

Streusel topping/filling
2 cups pecans, chopped
⅓ cup brown sugar
3 tablespoons sugar
1 teaspoon cinnamon

Cake
½ cup margarine
1 cup sugar
2 eggs
2 cups flour
1½ teaspoons baking powder
½ teaspoon soda
½ teaspoon salt
1 cup sour cream
1 teaspoon vanilla
2 cups fresh peaches, peeled
   and sliced

Combine all streusel ingredients; set aside. In large mixing bowl, cream margarine and sugar until fluffy. Beat in eggs. Combine all dry ingredients; add alternately with the sour cream and vanilla to the creamed mixture. Beat until smooth. Pour half the batter into a 9 inch springform pan. Sprinkle with 1 cup of streusel. Top with remaining batter and ½ cup streusel. Bake at 350° for 30 minutes. Arrange peaches over cake; sprinkle with remaining streusel. Bake an additional 30 to 40 minutes or until cake tests done. Cool cake 10 minutes before removing sides of pan. Serve warm or at room temperature. Serves 10

It takes 84 muscles to frown and only seven to smile.

Raspberry Cream Cheese Coffee Cake

2¼ cups flour
¾ cup sugar
¾ cup margarine
½ teaspoon baking powder
½ teaspoon soda
½ teaspoon salt
¾ cup sour cream
1 egg, beaten
1½ teaspoons almond extract
½ teaspoon vanilla

Filling
1 (8 ounce) package cream
    cheese, softened
½ cup sugar
1 egg
½ cup raspberry jam
½ cup slivered almonds

In large mixing bowl, combine flour and sugar. Cut in margarine as for pastry. Remove 1 cup and set aside. To remaining crumbs, add baking powder, soda, salt, sour cream, egg, vanilla and almond extract; mix well. Spread in bottom and 2 inches up the sides of a 9 inch spring-form pan. For filling, beat cream cheese, sugar and egg in small bowl; mix well. Pour over batter; spoon raspberry jam on top. Sprinkle with almonds and reserved crumbs. Bake at 350° for 55 to 60 minutes. Let stand 15 minutes before removing sides from pan. Serves 10

Apple Bread

2 cups apples, grated
1 cup sugar
1 teaspoon cinnamon
1½ cups flour
1 teaspoon soda
½ teaspoon salt
1 egg, beaten
½ cup oil
1 cup nuts, chopped

Mix apples, sugar and cinnamon together and set aside for 1 hour. Mix dry ingredients. Add egg and oil to apple mixture. Stir in dry ingredients and nuts. Pour in greased loaf pan and bake at 350° for 45 minutes.

Cranberry Orange Bread

2 cups flour
1½ teaspoons baking powder
1 teaspoon soda
½ teaspoon salt
1 cup sugar
1 egg, beaten
½ cup orange juice
Grated rind of 1 orange
2 tablespoons margarine,
   melted
2 tablespoons hot water
1 cup whole cranberries, raw
1 cup walnuts, chopped

Combine flour, baking powder, soda, salt and sugar in large mixing bowl; set aside. Mix beaten egg with orange juice, rind, margarine and hot water. Fold flour mixture into egg mixture until blended. Do not beat. Gently fold in cranberries and walnuts. Spoon into greased loaf pan or smaller pans of choice. Bake at 325° for 60 minutes; test in center with wooden pick. Cool on rack for 15 minutes before removing from pans.

Applesauce Bread

2 cups flour
1 teaspoon soda
½ teaspoon baking powder
½ teaspoon cinnamon
½ teaspoon nutmeg
½ teaspoon salt
1 cup sugar
1 (16 ounce) can applesauce
⅓ cup oil
2 tablespoons milk
2 eggs
¾ cup walnuts, chopped

Topping
¼ cup brown sugar
⅓ cup walnuts, chopped

Mix dry ingredients and set aside. In medium bowl combine sugar, applesauce, oil, milk and eggs; beat well. Stir in dry ingredients, combine well with as few strokes as possible. Stir in walnuts. Pour batter in greased bundt pan. Sprinkle combined topping ingredients over batter. Bake at 350° for 1 hour, covering loosely with foil after first ½ hour. Remove from pan after 10 minutes and cool on rack. Serve with whipped butter and honey. *Delicious!*

Mom's Cornbread

1 egg
1 cup whipping cream
1 cup buttermilk
½ teaspoon soda
½ teaspoon salt
Cornmeal to thicken

Mix first five ingredients together. Stir in enough cornmeal to thicken. (About cake batter consistency.) Bake at 450° in greased 9 x 13 inch pan or muffin tin for 20 to 25 minutes or until golden brown. Great with soups and pinto beans. *This recipe has been in our family for many years. We remember having this at Grandma's house when we were kids.*

Spanish Cornbread

1 cup cornmeal
¼ cup sugar
1 teaspoon salt
1 cup flour
3 teaspoons baking powder
1 egg
1 cup milk
¼ cup shortening
1 (small) can creamed corn
1 cup cottage cheese

Filling
½ cup green chilies
½ pound Cheddar cheese,
    grated

Combine dry ingredients, add egg, milk, shortening, corn and cottage cheese. Stir lightly. Pour half into greased 9 x 9-inch pan, add alternating layers of filling. Add remaining batter. Bake at 425° for 45 minutes.

Salads

Spinach Salad

Dressing
½ cup brown sugar
½ cup salad oil
⅓ cup vinegar
⅓ cup ketchup
1 tablespoon Worcestershire
    sauce

Salad
2 quarts fresh spinach
    leaves, torn
2 cups fresh bean sprouts
1 (8 ounce) can water
    chestnuts, sliced and
    drained
4 hard-cooked eggs, peeled
    and diced
6 slices bacon, fried and
    crumbled
1 small onion, thinly sliced

In a bottle or jar, combine all dressing ingredients. Shake well to mix. Set aside. In large salad bowl, toss salad ingredients. Just before serving, pour dressing over salad and toss. Serves 8

Strawberry Spinach Salad

2 bunches fresh spinach,
    washed and dried
1 pint fresh strawberries,
    sliced

Dressing
½ cup sugar
2 tablespoons sesame seeds
1 tablespoon poppy seeds
1½ teaspoons onion,
    chopped
¼ teaspoon Worcestershire
    sauce
¼ teaspoon paprika
½ cup vegetable oil
¼ cup vinegar

Arrange spinach and strawberries in large salad bowl. Place next six ingredients in blender or food processor. With unit running, add oil and vinegar in steady stream. Blend until thickened. Drizzle over salad; serve immediately. Serves 6 to 8

Layered Spinach Salad

¾ pound fresh spinach
½ medium cucumber, thinly
　sliced
½ cup radishes, thinly sliced
¼ cup green onions, thinly
　sliced
2 hard-cooked eggs, sliced
¾ cup Ranch style salad
　dressing
5 slices bacon, fried and
　crumbled
½ cup Spanish peanuts

Remove and discard spinach stems. Rinse leaves well; drain and pat dry. Cut spinach into bite sized pieces and arrange evenly in salad bowl. Evenly layer cucumber slices, radishes, green onions and eggs. Spread dressing over top. Cover; chill up to 24 hours. Just before serving, sprinkle with bacon and peanuts. Serves 6

Cooked Cranberry-Orange Relish

1 pound cranberries, washed
2 cups sugar
½ cup water
½ cup orange juice
2 teaspoons orange rind,
　grated
½ cup blanched almonds,
　slivered

Combine all ingredients, except almonds, in saucepan and cook until cranberries pop open, about 10 minutes. Skim foam from surface and cool. Stir in almonds just before serving. This can be made a day or two ahead and refrigerated. Bring to room temperature before serving. Great with ham or turkey.

Cranberry Orange Salad

1 cup sugar
½ cup walnuts, chopped
1 (12 ounce) package
　cranberries, fresh or
　frozen, finely chopped
1 (11 ounce) can mandarin
　oranges, drained
1 (6 ounce) package orange
　flavor gelatin
2 cups boiling water

In large bowl, combine sugar, walnuts, cranberries and oranges; set aside. In large bowl, dissolve gelatin in boiling water. Refrigerate until slightly thickened, about 45 minutes. Stir cranberry-orange mixture into thickened gelatin. Refrigerate about 3 hours in mold of your choice. To serve, unmold onto platter, garnish as desired. Serves 8

Norwegian Coleslaw

1 medium head cabbage
1 tablespoon salt
1½ cups sugar
1 cup vinegar
1 teaspoon mustard seed
1 teaspoon celery seed
2 cups celery, chopped
1 small green bell pepper,
    chopped
1 small red bell pepper,
    chopped
2 carrots, grated

Shred cabbage and toss with salt. Cover and refrigerate at least 2 hours. In saucepan, heat sugar, vinegar, mustard and celery seeds. Cook until sugar dissolves, about 10 minutes. Cool completely. Add to cabbage along with remaining vegetables; toss. Cover and refrigerate at least 1 week before serving. Keeps for 4 to 6 weeks in refrigerator. Serves 12 to 16

Chicken Pecan Salad

6 cups cooked chicken,
    cubed
1 cup celery, chopped
1 cup mayonnaise
1 cup lowfat yogurt
2 tablespoons lemon juice
¼ teaspoon salt
5 slices bacon, fried and
    crumbled
1 cup pecans, toasted
Lettuce leaves
Tomato wedges

In mixing bowl, combine chicken and celery. In another bowl, combine mayonnaise, yogurt, lemon juice and salt. Pour dressing over chicken; toss well to coat. Refrigerate. Just before serving, toss with bacon and pecans. Serve on lettuce with tomato garnish. Serves 6 to 8

Success is having the courage to meet failure without being defeated.

Fruit and Chicken Salad

Dressing
1 (8 ounce) carton lemon
    yogurt
2 tablespoons honey
1 teaspoon orange peel,
    grated

Salad
Leaf lettuce
2 apples, cut into wedges
2 cups cooked chicken,
    cubed
1 cup seedless red grapes,
    halved
½ cup celery, sliced
2 tablespoons walnuts,
    chopped

Arrange lettuce on plates. Fan apple wedges over lettuce. Mix chicken, grapes and celery. Add dressing and toss to coat. Spoon chicken over apples and sprinkle with walnuts. This is a wonderful salad, serve with fresh bread or rolls for a great lunch. Serves 4 to 6

Chicken Salad

2½ cups cooked chicken,
    cubed
4 slices bacon, fried and
    crumbled
1 (8 ounce) can sliced water
    chestnuts, drained
½ cup celery, sliced
1 cup green grapes, halved

Dressing
¾ cup mayonnaise
1 to 2 tablespoons parsley
    flakes
2 teaspoons onions, chopped
1 teaspoon lemon juice
⅓ teaspoon ginger
Dash of Worcestershire
    sauce

Mix all salad ingredients. Mix dressing and stir into salad. Refrigerate. Serve on beds of lettuce.

Bean Salad

1 (16 ounce) can cut green
  beans
2 (17 ounce) cans lima beans
1 (16 ounce) can kidney
  beans
1 (16 ounce) can wax beans
1 (15 ounce) can garbanzo
  beans
1 large green pepper,
  chopped
3 celery stalks, chopped
1 bunch green onions, sliced

Dressing
2 cups vinegar
2 cups sugar
½ cup water
1 tablespoon salt

Drain all beans; place in large bowl. Add green pepper, celery, and green onions; set aside. Bring remaining ingredients to a boil in heavy saucepan; boil for 5 minutes. Remove from heat and immediately pour over vegetables. Refrigerate several hours or overnight. Serves 14

Bean Salad Dressing

¾ cup vinegar
¾ cup salad oil
1 cup sugar
½ teaspoon salt
¼ teaspoon pepper

Mix all together and serve over bean salad.

We never know where God hides His pools. God leads me into the hard places, and then I find I have gone into the dwelling place of eternal springs.

Rhubarb Salad

3 cups rhubarb, fresh or
   frozen, sliced
1 tablespoon sugar
1 (3 ounce) package
   raspberry gelatin
1 cup pineapple juice,
   unsweetened
1 teaspoon lemon juice
1 cup apples, peeled and
   diced
1 cup celery, diced
¼ cup pecans, chopped

In medium saucepan, cook and stir rhubarb and sugar over medium-low heat until rhubarb is soft and tender. Remove from heat; add gelatin and stir until dissolved. Stir in pineapple and lemon juices. Chill until partially set. Stir in apples, celery and pecans. Pour into Jello mold. Chill several hours or overnight. Serves 8

Strawberry Rhubarb Salad

4 cups fresh rhubarb, diced
1½ cups water
½ cup sugar
1 (6 ounce) package
   strawberry Jello
1 cup orange juice
1 teaspoon orange rind,
   grated
1 cup fresh strawberries,
   sliced

Combine rhubarb, water and sugar in saucepan. Cook and stir over medium heat until rhubarb is tender. Remove from heat; add gelatin and stir until dissolved. Add orange juice and rind. Chill until syrupy. Add strawberries. Pour into 6 cup mold. Chill until set. This is a wonderful and refreshing salad in the springtime. Serves 8 to 10

Rehearse your troubles to God only.

Layered Pea Salad

½ head of lettuce, shredded
6 green onions, chopped
1 cup celery, chopped
1 medium green bell pepper,
    chopped
1 medium red bell pepper,
    chopped
1 (10 ounce) package frozen
    peas, thawed
4 hard-boiled eggs, sliced
¾ cup Ranch style dressing
4 ounces Cheddar cheese,
    grated
8 slices bacon, fried and
    crumbled

Put lettuce in bottom of bowl. Layer onions, celery, peppers, peas, and eggs. Spread dressing on top of eggs. Sprinkle cheese and bacon on top of dressing. *This is a very pretty salad in a clear bowl and is great for spring or any time of year. This is a family favorite!*

Crunchy Pea Salad

1 (10 ounce) package frozen
    peas, thawed
1 cup celery, diced
1 cup cauliflower, chopped
¼ cup green onions, chopped
1 cup cashews, chopped
½ cup plain yogurt
1 cup Ranch dressing
4 slices bacon, fried and
    crumbled

Combine all ingredients. Chill. Garnish with bacon. Excellent salad!

It is such a comfort to drop the tangles of life into God's hands and leave them there.

Creamy Avocado Zucchini Salad

½ cup sour cream
¼ cup mayonnaise
2 tablespoons milk
1 teaspoon salt
½ teaspoon Italian
    seasonings
⅛ teaspoon garlic salt
3 medium avocados, diced
3 medium zucchini, sliced

Combine cream, mayonnaise, milk and seasonings. Gently stir in avocados and zucchini until well mixed. Chill before serving. *This salad is a wonderful way to help you use all your extra squash in summer.* Serves 8

Cranberry Salad

1 (12 ounce) package
    cranberries, ground
1½ cups sugar
¼ cup miniature
    marshmallows
¾ cup grapes, halved
¼ cup crushed pineapple,
    drained
¼ cup nuts, chopped
¾ cup frozen whipped
    topping, thawed
¼ cup mayonnaise

Mix sugar and cranberries together and let stand for at least 24 hours in refrigerator. Add other ingredients, except whipped topping and mayonnaise. Mix whipped topping and mayonnaise together and stir into salad. Excellent salad for any holiday. *This recipe has been in our family for a long time. It was given to us years ago by a favorite aunt.*

7-Up Jello Salad

1 (3 ounce) package orange
    Jello
1 cup 7-Up
1 cup orange juice
1 (6 ounce) can crushed
    pineapple, drained
¾ cup pecans, chopped

In saucepan bring to boil, orange Jello, 7-Up and orange juice. Stir until Jello dissolves. Mix in pineapple and pecans. Chill until set. *If you like Jello salad, you will love this.*

Frog Eye Salad

1 cup sugar
2 tablespoons flour
2½ teaspoons salt
3 quarts water
1¾ cups pineapple juice
2 eggs, beaten
1 tablespoon lemon juice
1 tablespoon cooking oil
1 (16 ounce) package Acini-
    De-Pepe
3 (11 ounce) cans mandarin
    oranges, drained
2 (20 ounce) cans pineapple
    chunks, drained
1 (20 ounce) can crushed
    pineapple, drained
1 (12 ounce) carton frozen
    whipped topping
1 cup miniature
    marshmallows

Combine sugar, flour and 1½ teaspoons salt. Gradually stir in pineapple juice and eggs. Cook over moderate heat, stirring until thick; add lemon juice. Cool. Bring water, 1 teaspoon salt and oil to boil. Add Acini-De-Pepe, cook at rolling boil until done. Drain and rinse twice. Combine egg mixture and Acini-De-Pepe. Refrigerate overnight in airtight container. Add remaining ingredients, toss lightly. May be kept for as long as a week. This is a great salad for a big group. Serves 25

Fruit Salad

1 cup mandarin oranges,
    drained
1 cup pineapple tidbits,
    drained
1 cup miniature
    marshmallows
1 cup coconut
1 cup sour cream
¼ cup maraschino cherries
    (optional)

Mix all together and refrigerate. Excellent and quick salad.

Rice and Asparagus Salad

1 (14 ounce) can chicken
    broth
1 cup long grain rice
1 (10 ounce) package frozen
    asparagus, cooked and
    drained
¾ cup peas
⅓ cup pecan halves or
    almonds
¼ cup parsley or cilantro
3 green onions, chopped

Dressing
4 tablespoons olive oil
½ teaspoon lemon peel
3 tablespoons lemon juice
3 tablespoons sour cream or
    yogurt
Spinach leaves

Cook rice in chicken broth until done. Cool. Add all other ingredients and toss with the dressing. This can be made with fresh asparagus also.

Oriental Cabbage Salad

1 (3 ounce) package Oriental
    noodles with chicken
    flavor
4 cups cabbage, shredded
4 green onions, sliced
2 tablespoons sesame seed
3 tablespoons vinegar
2 tablespoons sugar
2 tablespoons salad oil
½ teaspoon pepper
¼ teaspoon salt
½ cup almonds, slivered

Crush noodles slightly, place in colander. Pour boiling water over noodles to soften slightly. Drain well. In large mixing bowl, combine noodles, cabbage, onions and sesame seed. For dressing, in a screw-top jar, combine seasoning packet from noodles, vinegar, sugar, oil, pepper and salt; shake well to mix. Pour over cabbage mixture and toss. Cover and chill several hours or overnight. Before serving, stir in almonds. (For a crunchier salad, do not soften noodles, use straight from package.) Serves 6 to 8

Oriental Noodle and Pasta Salad

1½ cups uncooked rotini
   (spiral macaroni)
1½ cups frozen sugar snap
   peas, thawed and drained
½ cup carrots, thinly sliced
3 red onion slices, quartered
⅓ cup oil
2 tablespoons sugar
1 (3 ounce) package instant
   Oriental noodles with
   Oriental flavor packet
1 tablespoon sesame seed,
   toasted

Cook rotini to desired doneness as directed on package. Drain; rinse with cold water. In large bowl, combine rotini, sugar snap peas, carrots and onions. In small bowl, combine oil, sugar and Oriental flavor packet; blend well. Pour over pasta mixture; toss to coat. Cover and refrigerate 1 hour to blend flavors. Just before serving, break Oriental noodles into pieces. Add noodle pieces and sesame seeds to salad; toss to combine. Serves 8

Mixed Green Vegetable Pasta Salad

Salad
2 cups uncooked mostaccioli
8 ounces fresh asparagus,
   cut into 2-inch pieces,
   cooked
1¾ cups zucchini, sliced
1 cup snow peas, blanched

Lemon Basil Dressing
¼ cup oil
¼ cup lemon juice
¼ cup fresh basil, chopped
   or ¼ teaspoon dried basil
1 teaspoon sugar
½ teaspoon salt
½ teaspoon pepper

Cook mostaccioli to desired doneness as directed on package. Drain; rinse with cold water. In large bowl, combine all salad ingredients; toss to combine. In jar with tight-fitting lid, combine all dressing ingredients; shake well. Pour dressing over salad; toss to combine. Serves 6

Chicken 'N Corn Tostada Salad

Dressing
¼ cup vinegar
3 tablespoons honey
1½ teaspoons cumin
¼ teaspoon salt
⅛ teaspoon pepper

Salad
1 tablespoon olive oil
2 whole chicken breasts,
    boneless and cut into
    2 x ½ inch strips
½ teaspoon garlic salt
1 (16 ounce) package frozen
    corn
1 cup tomatoes, chopped
1 (15 ounce) can black beans,
    drained and rinsed
2 green onions, sliced
2 avocados, chopped
1 head lettuce, torn into bite
    sized pieces
1 small red bell pepper,
    chopped
2 cups Monterey Jack
    cheese, grated
3 cups blue corn tortilla chips
    or tortilla chips, crushed

Garnish
1¼ cups salsa
1¼ cups sour cream

In small jar with tight-fitting lid, combine all dressing ingredients; shake well. Set aside. Heat oil in large skillet over medium-high heat until hot. Add chicken; cook until no longer pink, about 5 minutes. Transfer chicken to very large bowl; sprinkle with garlic salt. Prepare corn according to package directions; drain. Stir into chicken. Cover and refrigerate about 30 minutes. Add tomatoes, black beans, onions, avocados, lettuce and red pepper to chicken mixture. Toss to combine. Shake dressing; pour over salad mixture; toss lightly. Just before serving, add cheese and tortilla chips; toss gently. Garnish with salsa and sour cream. Serve immediately. Serves 10

 Success is being better tomorrow than you are today.

Warm Chicken and Corn Salad

Dressing
⅓ cup lemon juice
⅓ cup olive oil
¼ cup green onions, chopped
1 tablespoon fresh cilantro,
     chopped
¼ teaspoon salt
⅛ teaspoon cayenne pepper

Salad
2 whole chicken breasts,
     skinned, boned and
     halved
2 cups corn, cooked and
     drained
½ cup red bell pepper, diced
½ cup green bell pepper,
     diced
Leaf lettuce
Lemon

In jar with tight-fitting lid, combine all dressing ingredients. Shake well. In medium glass bowl, combine half of dressing and chicken; turn to coat. Marinate ½ hour. Prepare charcoal fire for grilling. In medium bowl, combine corn, red pepper and green peppers. Pour remaining dressing over corn mixture. Toss gently. Grill chicken until done or juices run clear. Brush with dressing during grilling. To serve, spoon corn mixture onto 4 lettuce lined plates. Slice chicken crosswise, do not separate slices. Transfer to serving plates with corn mixture. Lightly squeeze fresh lemon juice over each salad. Garnish with cilantro. *Wonderful salad!* Serves 4

Broccoli Salad

5 cups fresh broccoli,
     chopped
½ cup raisins
¼ cup green onion, sliced
2 tablespoons sugar
3 tablespoons vinegar
1 cup mayonnaise
10 bacon slices, fried and
     crumbled
1 cup sunflower seeds

In large salad bowl, combine broccoli, raisins and onions. In small bowl, combine sugar, vinegar and mayonnaise. Pour over broccoli; toss to coat. Refrigerate. Just before serving sprinkle with bacon and sunflower seeds; toss. This salad is a crowd pleaser! Serves 6 to 8

Barley, Corn and Pepper Salad

Salad
1 cup uncooked barley
2 cups frozen corn, thawed
   and drained
½ cup red bell pepper, diced
½ cup green bell pepper,
   diced
½ cup green onions, sliced

Cilantro Dressing
⅓ cup olive oil
⅓ cup lemon juice
¼ cup chopped fresh cilantro
½ teaspoon salt
Coarsely ground black
   pepper

Cook barley to desired doneness as directed on package. Drain; rinse with cold water. In large bowl, combine all salad ingredients; toss well. In jar with tight-fitting lid, combine all dressing ingredients; shake well. Pour dressing over salad; toss to combine. Serve at room temperature or chill. Store in refrigerator. Serves 8

Chicken and Pasta Toss

1½ cups corkscrew macaroni
2 cups fresh spinach, cut
1½ cups cooked chicken,
   diced
8 cherry tomatoes, halved
1 cup fresh mushrooms,
   sliced
¼ cup Parmesan cheese,
   grated
⅓ cup olive oil
3 tablespoons Dijon mustard
1 tablespoon lemon juice
¼ teaspoon garlic salt
⅛ teaspoon pepper

Cook macaroni according to package directions; drain. Rinse under cold water; drain. In medium salad bowl, combine pasta, spinach, chicken, cherry tomatoes, mushrooms and Parmesan cheese. In small bowl whisk together oil, mustard, lemon juice, garlic salt, and pepper until smooth. Pour over pasta mixture. Toss lightly. Serve immediately. Serves 4

Pasta Salad

1 pound linguini broken into
   thirds, cooked
2 cucumbers, chopped
3 tomatoes, chopped
1 green bell pepper, chopped
1 red bell pepper, chopped
1 cup olives, sliced
1 cup pepperoni, chopped
1 jar Schilling's salad
   seasonings
1 small bottle Italian dressing

Cook linguini. Drain; rinse with cold water. Add other ingredients. Refrigerate. Serve with Parmesan cheese. Excellent salad. *This is a great salad for family gatherings.*

Layered Spinach Pasta Salad

1 (9 ounce) package
   refrigerated uncooked
   cheese tortellini
2 cups red cabbage,
   shredded
6 cups spinach leaves, torn
1 cup cherry tomatoes,
   halved
½ cup green onions, sliced
1 (8 ounce) bottle prepared
   Ranch dressing
8 slices bacon, fried and
   crumbled

Cook tortellini to desired doneness as directed on package. Drain; rinse with cold water. In large glass bowl with straight sides or a 9 x 13 inch baking dish, layer cabbage, spinach, tortellini, tomatoes and green onions. Pour dressing evenly over top; sprinkle with bacon. Cover; refrigerate until serving time. *This is a great summertime salad, so good with meat cooked on grill.* Serves 8

Success does not come in one large mass, but is indeed a multitude of daily mini successes.

Strawberries and Asparagus Elegante

Dressing
¼ cup lemon juice
2 tablespoons oil
2 tablespoons honey

Salad
2 cups fresh asparagus
　spears, cut into 1-inch
　pieces
2 cups fresh strawberries,
　sliced

In jar with tight-fitting lid, combine lemon juice, oil and honey; shake well. Partially cook asparagus in rapidly boiling water for 3 to 5 minutes or until crisp-tender; drain. Rinse with cold water. Arrange asparagus and strawberries on 4 individual salad plates. Drizzle with dressing. *Not only is this pretty, it's yummy!* Serves 4

Pretzel Strawberry Salad

1 (6 ounce) package
　strawberry Jello
1 (16 ounce) package frozen
　strawberries, thawed
2½ cups boiling water
2 cups crushed pretzels
2 tablespoons sugar
½ cup margarine, melted
1 (8 ounce) package cream
　cheese, softened
2 cups frozen whipped
　topping, thawed
1 cup sugar

Mix Jello and boiling water together, add strawberries with liquid. Refrigerate until partially set. Mix pretzels, sugar and margarine together; put in bottom of 9 x 13 inch pan. Bake at 350° for 8 to 10 minutes. Cool. Mix together cream cheese, sugar and whipped topping. Spread over cooled crust, chill until firm. Pour partially set Jello mixture over cream cheese mixture. Chill until firm. *This is a yummy salad.*

Success is relative, individual and personal.

Trifle Fruit Salad

2 cups fresh pineapple
chunks
2 cups strawberries, sliced
2 cups blueberries
2 cups seedless green
grapes

Topping
1¼ cups milk
½ cup sour cream
1 (3¾ ounce) package instant
vanilla cream pudding
and pie filling mix
1 (8 ounce) can crushed
pineapple, undrained

In trifle bowl or large glass serving bowl, layer fruits. In medium bowl, combine milk and sour cream; blend well. Add pudding mix; beat until well blended, about 2 minutes. Stir in pineapple. Spoon pudding mixture over fruit to within 1 inch of edge. Cover; refrigerate several hours to blend flavors. Garnish as desired. *This fruit salad is wonderful and what a pretty presentation!* Serves 10

Fruit Salad Dressing

1¼ cups milk
½ cup sour cream
1 (3¾ ounce) package instant
vanilla pudding
1 (8 ounce) can crushed
pineapple, undrained

Mix all together and pour over fruit salad. Store in refrigerator.

Honey Mustard Salad Dressing

½ cup vinegar
1 cup mayonnaise
1 teaspoon prepared mustard
1 teaspoon sugar
1 teaspoon onion, finely
chopped
½ cup honey
1 teaspoon parsley, minced
¼ teaspoon salt
¼ teaspoon pepper
½ cup vegetable oil

In small bowl, combine vinegar, mayonnaise and mustard. Add sugar, onion, honey, parsley, salt and pepper. Slowly pour oil into mixture while mixing briskly with wire whisk. (Can make in blender or food processor.) Refrigerate until ready to serve. Makes 2 cups

Vegetables, Pasta & Rice

Picnic Peas

1 tablespoon oil
1 cup green bell pepper,
   chopped
1 cup onion, chopped
1 cup celery, sliced
1 tablespoon sugar
1 bay leaf
1 (15 ounce) can black-eyed
   peas, drained and rinsed
1 (14 ounce) can tomatoes,
   chopped, liquid reserved
½ teaspoon salt
¼ teaspoon pepper
4 bacon slices, fried and
   crumbled

In skillet heat oil and sauté peppers, onions and celery. Add sugar, bay leaf, peas, tomatoes, half tomato liquid, salt and pepper Reduce heat and simmer 15 minutes. Remove to bowl and sprinkle with bacon. Serve hot or at room temperature. This is a great picnic salad. It goes good with hot dogs or hamburgers. Serves 6

French Peas

2 green onions, chopped
1 cup lettuce, finely shredded
1 tablespoon oil
1 teaspoon flour
¼ cup water
1 (10 ounce) package frozen
   or fresh peas, cooked
1 (8 ounce) can sliced water
   chestnuts, drained
Dash of black pepper

In saucepan, sauté onions and lettuce in oil for 5 minutes. Set aside. Combine flour with water; add to onion mixture and cook, stirring until thickened. Add peas, water chestnuts and seasonings. Serves 8

If you are ever to be strong in the Lord and the power of His might, your strength will be born in some storm.

Festive Peas and Mushrooms

2 tablespoons margarine
2½ cups fresh mushrooms,
   sliced
2 cups frozen peas
1 (8 ounce) can sliced water
   chestnuts, drained
1 (2 ounce) jar sliced
   pimiento, drained
Salt
Pepper

In large skillet, melt margarine; add mushrooms and sauté 1 minute. Add peas, water chestnuts and pimiento. Cover; cook over medium heat 3 to 5 minutes or until peas are tender. Add salt and pepper to taste. This is great with roast beef. Serves 6

Spicy Rice Casserole

1 pound mild bulk pork
   sausage
1 teaspoon cumin
1 clove garlic, minced
2 medium onions, chopped
2 medium green bell peppers,
   chopped
2 beef bouillon cubes
2 cups boiling water
1 to 2 jalapeño peppers,
   seeded and finely
   chopped
1 (6¼ ounce) package long
   grain and wild rice

In large skillet, cook sausage, cumin and garlic, stirring often. Drain. Add onions and peppers; sauté until crisp-tender. Dissolve bouillon in water; add to skillet. Stir in jalapeños, rice and rice seasoning packet; bring to boil. Reduce heat and simmer, uncovered, 5 to 10 minutes or until water is absorbed. This is a great side dish or serve with a salad and cornbread as a main dish. Serves 4

Cashew Rice

1 (8 ounce) can cashews
2 (16 ounce) cans beef
   bouillon
1½ cups uncooked regular
   rice
1 green bell pepper, chopped
1 onion, chopped
1 cup mushrooms, sliced
3 tablespoons margarine

Sauté onions and peppers in margarine. Add rice, bouillon, mushrooms, cashews and mix well. Pour in 2 quart casserole dish. Cover. Bake at 375° for approximately 45 minutes or until liquid is absorbed and rice is tender. Serves 6

Spanish Rice

1 cup rice
2 tablespoons bacon
   drippings
1 onion, chopped
1 to 2 cloves garlic, minced
1 (16 ounce) can stewed
   tomatoes
½ teaspoon pepper
½ teaspoon chili powder
½ teaspoon cumin
1 teaspoon salt
1½ cups water

Heat bacon drippings in skillet, add rice and cook until it starts to brown. Add onions and garlic to rice, cook for 2 to 3 minutes. Add other ingredients, cover and simmer until tender, about 20 to 30 minutes. This is wonderful with Mexican food. Serves 4

Wild Rice and Apricots

3 cups cooked wild rice
4 tablespoons margarine,
   melted
4 tablespoons fresh parsley,
   chopped
2 tablespoons onion,
   chopped
¾ cup celery, sliced
¾ cup dried apricots,
   chopped
⅛ teaspoon thyme
⅛ teaspoon mace
⅛ teaspoon nutmeg
⅛ teaspoon cloves
1 teaspoon black pepper
½ teaspoon salt

While rice is cooking, melt margarine in small skillet and sauté onions until transparent, add parsley, celery and apricots. While rice is hot, combine with all ingredients, toss and serve warm. Serves 6

Veggie Rice

2 cups cooked rice, any kind
1 cup zucchini, sliced
¾ cup green onions, sliced
1 (7 ounce) can corn, drained
   or 1 cup frozen corn
1 tablespoon parsley
¼ teaspoon thyme
¼ teaspoon garlic powder
⅛ teaspoon pepper

Spray large nonstick skillet with cooking spray. Sauté zucchini and onions 3 to 5 minutes, stirring occasionally. Stir in rice, corn and seasonings. Cover, simmer over low heat 5 to 10 minutes to blend flavors. Serves 4

Confetti Spaghetti

1 cup pepperoni slices
½ cup onion, chopped
½ cup green bell pepper
   strips
1 (8 ounce) package
   spaghetti, cooked and
   drained
½ cup Parmesan cheese
½ cup mozzarella cheese,
   grated
½ cup tomato, chopped
½ teaspoon oregano

Fry pepperoni in large skillet until edges curl. Add onion and peppers; cook until tender. Toss together cooked spaghetti, cheeses, tomato and oregano; add pepperoni, onions and peppers. Heat thoroughly. Sprinkle with additional Parmesan cheese, if desired. Serves 4

Quick and Easy Tortellini

1 (14 ounce) package
   uncooked cheese filled
   tortellini
2 tablespoons olive oil
1 clove garlic, minced
¼ cup white wine
¼ teaspoon salt
⅛ teaspoon pepper
¼ cup fresh parsley, chopped

Cook tortellini to desired doneness as directed on package. Drain; rinse with hot water. Keep warm. Heat oil in large skillet over medium heat. Add garlic; cook 2 minutes, stirring constantly. Stir in wine, salt, pepper and tortellini. Reduce heat to low; simmer over low heat 5 minutes or until thoroughly heated. Toss with parsley. Serves 6

Parsley Noodles

1 (8 ounce) package
   uncooked wide egg
   noodles
¼ cup margarine
1 tablespoon fresh parsley,
   chopped
½ teaspoon salt
Dash pepper

Cook noodles to desired doneness as directed on package, drain. In large saucepan, melt margarine over low heat. Stir in cooked noodles, parsley, salt and pepper. Continue cooking until thoroughly heated, stirring constantly. Serves 4

Seeded Bowtie Noodles

8 ounces bowtie noodles
3 tablespoons margarine
1 teaspoon poppyseeds
½ teaspoon salt
¼ teaspoon pepper

Cook noodles according to package directions, about 15 minutes. Drain; toss gently with remaining ingredients. Serves 4

Noodles and Asparagus

4 cups uncooked wide egg
   noodles
2 cups fresh asparagus,
   cut up
⅓ cup butter

Cook noodles to desired doneness as directed on package. Drain. Return noodles to saucepan; keep warm. Meanwhile, cook asparagus in boiling water for 3 to 5 minutes or until crisp-tender. Drain. Add to noodles; keep warm. In small saucepan over low heat, heat butter until light golden brown, stirring constantly. Pour butter over noodles and asparagus; toss to coat. Serves 4

Pasta Primavera

1 pound ground Italian
   sausage
1 cup mushrooms, fresh and
   sliced
3 tablespoons margarine
3 tablespoons olive oil
¼ teaspoon garlic powder
⅓ cup green onions, sliced
1 zucchini, sliced
1 green bell pepper, cut in
   strips
1 teaspoon parsley
½ teaspoon basil
½ teaspoon oregano
12 ounces fettucini noodles
   or linguini
3 tablespoons margarine
1 cup whipping cream
⅔ cup Parmesan cheese

Cook sausage in skillet until browned. Drain and set aside in a bowl. In same skillet, sauté mushrooms in 3 tablespoons margarine. Put mushrooms in bowl with sausage. Add oil to skillet and sauté garlic and onions. Stir in zucchini, peppers, parsley, basil and oregano. Cook until vegetables are crisp-tender. Stir in sausage and mushrooms. While vegetables are cooking, cook fettucini in boiling salted water according to directions. Drain. In large saucepan, heat 3 tablespoons margarine with whipping cream (do not boil). When thoroughly heated, stir in cooked fettucini and Parmesan cheese. Pour onto large platter and top with vegetables and sausage mixture. Serve immediately. You can grill chicken breasts or cook shrimp instead of sausage. This dish is so versatile because you can use so many different vegetables - mushrooms, broccoli, carrots, celery or whatever you like.

God will not look you over for medals, degrees or diplomas, but for scars.

Lemon Dijon Pasta and Peas

2 cups uncooked dried pasta
   nuggets
2 cups frozen peas
1 tablespoon margarine
1 tablespoon flour
¼ teaspoon salt
⅛ teaspoon pepper
1 cup milk
2 tablespoons Dijon mustard
1 tablespoon onion, chopped
2 teaspoons lemon juice

Cook pasta according to package directions, adding peas during last 5 minutes of cooking. Drain, rinse with hot water. Meanwhile, in 3-quart saucepan melt margarine until sizzling; stir in flour, salt and pepper until smooth and bubbly (1 minute). Gradually stir in milk and mustard. Cook over medium heat, stirring constantly, until mixture comes to a full boil (4 to 6 minutes); boil 1 minute. Remove from heat; stir in onion and lemon juice. Immediately add pasta mixture; toss to coat with sauce. Serves 6

Green Chili Scalloped Corn

1 tablespoon margarine
1 tablespoon onion, chopped
½ teaspoon red pepper flakes
1 tablespoon flour
⅓ cup Parmesan cheese
1 (15 ounce) can cream style
   corn
1 (4 ounce) can green chilies,
   diced
2 eggs, beaten

In medium saucepan melt margarine. Add onion and red pepper flakes, cook until tender. Stir in flour, cook 1 minute, stirring constantly. Remove from heat. Reserve 1 tablespoon of cheese. Stir remaining cheese, corn, chilies and eggs into flour mixture. Pour into greased 1½ quart casserole dish. Sprinkle reserved cheese over top. Bake at 350° for 45 to 50 minutes or until knife inserted near center comes out clean. Serves 4

Asparagus Au Gratin

1¼ pounds fresh asparagus
2 tablespoons margarine
2 tablespoons onion,
    chopped
2 tablespoons flour
½ teaspoon salt
⅛ teaspoon pepper
Dash of ground nutmeg
⅔ cup chicken broth
⅓ cup half-and-half
Toast points
Margarine
½ cup Cheddar cheese,
    grated

Clean and cook asparagus in small amount of boiling water until crisp-tender, about 3 to 4 minutes. Drain; set aside. In medium saucepan, melt margarine; stir in onion, cook until transparent. Stir in flour, salt, pepper and nutmeg over low heat until smooth. Stir in broth and cream; cook until thickened, stirring constantly. Set aside. Butter toast points; place under preheated broiler until golden brown. Remove to a 9 x 13 inch baking dish. Place asparagus over bread; pour sauce over all. Sprinkle with cheese. Bake at 400° for 8 to 10 minutes until cheese melts. Serves 4

Stir-Fried Asparagus

2 pounds fresh asparagus,
    cut into 1 inch pieces
1 tablespoon cornstarch
½ cup chicken broth
1 tablespoon dry sherry
1 tablespoon soy sauce
1 teaspoon vinegar
¼ teaspoon dry mustard
3 tablespoons oil
¼ teaspoon sugar
¼ teaspoon salt
1 clove garlic, minced

Blend cornstarch and chicken broth in small bowl; stir in the sherry, soy sauce, vinegar, sugar and mustard. In large skillet, heat 3 tablespoons oil until hot, but not smoking. Add asparagus and stir quickly. Sprinkle with salt and garlic. Continue to stir 3 to 4 minutes until crisp-tender. Stir in cornstarch mixture and continue stir-frying 1 more minute until it thickens slightly and coats asparagus. You can use any fresh veggie for this dish. Serves 6

Stir-Fried Oriental Broccoli

2 tablespoons oil
3 cups broccoli florets, cut
   into 1 inch pieces
1 onion, chopped
¼ cup water
1 (8 ounce) can bamboo
   shoots, sliced and
   drained
1 cup mushrooms, sliced
2 tablespoons almonds,
   slivered
2 tablespoons soy sauce
1 tablespoon pimiento

In large skillet or wok, heat oil over high heat. Add broccoli and onion; stir to coat with oil. Add water; stir-fry over high heat 3 to 5 minutes or until broccoli is crisp-tender. Add remaining ingredients; stir-fry until heated thoroughly. Serve immediately. Serves 8

Broccoli and Cheese Bake

2 eggs
1 cup cottage cheese
1 cup American cheese,
   grated
3 tablespoons flour
Paprika
2 teaspoons salt
¼ teaspoon onion powder
2 (10 ounce) packages frozen
   broccoli, chopped and
   thawed
1 (8 ounce) can water
   chestnuts, sliced

Beat eggs. Beat in cheese, flour, salt and onion powder. Stir broccoli and water chestnuts into egg mixture. Pour into greased 9 inch pan. Sprinkle with paprika. Bake at 350° for 30 to 35 minutes or until mixture is firm. Serves 6

Broccoli Casserole

1 (10 ounce) package
   broccoli, chopped
1 cup rice, uncooked
½ cup onion, chopped
1 cup celery, sliced
½ cup margarine
1 (8 ounce) jar processed
   cheese
1 (15 ounce) can cream of
   chicken soup

Cook rice as directed. Sauté onions, celery, and broccoli in margarine. Combine all ingredients and bake at 350° for 20 to 30 minutes. This dish freezes well. (Freeze before baking.) Serves 6

Green Beans With Walnut Sauce

2 pounds fresh green beans,
   leave whole
4 cups ice cubes
1 quart water

Sauce
¼ cup walnuts, chopped
¼ cup fresh parsley, chopped
2 green onions, cut in 1 inch
   pieces
¼ teaspoon salt
⅛ teaspoon pepper
⅓ cup mayonnaise
2 tablespoons lemon juice
½ cup oil
1 (2 ounce) jar diced
   pimiento, drained

Cook beans until crisp-tender, plunge in ice water to stop cooking. In blender or processor, combine nuts, parsley, onions, salt, pepper, mayonnaise and lemon juice. Process until smooth. With machine running, pour oil in thin stream to make thick sauce. Arrange beans on platter and pour sauce over them. Sprinkle with pimientos. This is a wonderful way to fix beans when your garden is doing "more than you dreamed!" Pick beans when small and tender. Serves 8

Mushroom and Italian Green Beans

2 (9 ounce) packages frozen
Italian green beans
1½ cups fresh mushrooms,
sliced
6 tablespoons margarine
½ teaspoon salt

Cook beans in boiling salted water for 5 minutes. Drain. Melt margarine in large skillet, sauté mushrooms. Add beans to mushrooms in skillet. Sprinkle with salt. Stir and let simmer 5 minutes. Cover with lid and remove from heat until serving time. Before serving, heat thoroughly again. (Better if made 1 hour ahead of serving to allow mushroom and bean flavors to blend.) Serves 4

Green Bean Casserole

2 packages frozen French
green beans
2 tablespoons margarine
½ cup onion, chopped
1 cup sour cream
½ cup almonds, sliced
½ pound Cheddar cheese,
grated

Cook and drain beans. Melt margarine and sauté onions. Add to beans. Add cheese. Fold in sour cream. Bake at 350° for 30 minutes. French fried onions may be added to top before baking. Serves 8

Remember that it is better to walk in the dark with God than to walk alone in the light.

Broiled Squash and Peppers

¼ cup margarine, melted
1 teaspoon oregano leaves
1 garlic clove, minced
½ teaspoon salt
¼ teaspoon pepper
6 small pattypan squash or 3
  medium zucchini or 3
  yellow squash, cut in half
  lengthwise
1 red or green bell pepper,
  cut into sixths, seeded
1 large onion, cut into sixths

In small bowl, combine margarine, oregano, garlic, salt and pepper; mix well. Put vegetables on pan for broiling. Broil 4 to 6 inches from heat for 8 minutes; turn vegetables over. Broil 4 to 6 minutes or until vegetables are crisp-tender. Brush with margarine mixture. Serves 6

Stir-Fry Summer Squash Medley

1 tablespoon oil
1 zucchini, cut into strips
2 summer squash, cut into
  strips
1 yellow crookneck or yellow
  Italian squash, cut on
  diagonal
1 red bell pepper, seeded and
  cut into strips
2 green onions, sliced
⅓ cup fresh dill, minced
1½ tablespoons freshly
  squeezed lemon juice
1 teaspoon lemon rind,
  grated
¼ teaspoon crushed red
  pepper flakes

Heat wok or large skillet, until very hot. Add oil. Watch carefully and as soon as oil begins to smoke, add squash, and stir-fry 6 minutes. Add peppers and onions, continue to stir-fry another 3 minutes. Add dill, lemon juice, lemon zest and red pepper. Toss to coat vegetables and stir-fry 1 minute. Serve immediately. Serves 4 to 6

Baked Squash

3 pounds yellow squash
½ cup onion, chopped
½ cup cracker crumbs
2 eggs
½ cup margarine
1 tablespoon sugar
1 teaspoon salt
½ teaspoon pepper

Wash and cut up squash. Boil until crisp-tender, drain thoroughly, then mash. Add all ingredients except ¼ cup margarine to squash. Melt remaining margarine, pour mixture in baking dish, then spread melted margarine over top and sprinkle with cracker crumbs. Bake at 375° for approximately 1 hour or until brown on top. Excellent dish. Serves 8

Squash Patties

2 cups zucchini squash,
   grated
⅓ cup biscuit mix
¼ cup Parmesan cheese
1 egg
Oil

Mix all ingredients except oil. Heat 1 to 2 tablespoons oil in skillet. Spoon squash mixture into small patties and fry until golden brown, turning once. Great way to help you use your excess zucchini. Serve hot. Serves 4

Squash Italian Style

2 pounds yellow squash, cut
   in half lengthwise
¼ cup bottled Italian salad
   dressing
½ teaspoon salt

In skillet over medium heat, combine salad dressing and squash, cut side down, cook about 5 minutes. Turn and sprinkle with salt. Reduce heat to low; cover and simmer 10 minutes or until crisp-tender. Serves 6

Scalloped Corn

4 cups corn
¾ cup soda cracker crumbs
1½ cups milk at room
    temperature
1 egg, beaten until frothy
2 tablespoons sugar
2 tablespoons margarine,
    melted
1 teaspoon salt
⅛ teaspoon pepper
Bread crumbs

In a greased 9 inch baking dish, layer half cracker crumbs, then half corn; layer remaining crumbs and corn. Combine milk, egg, sugar, margarine, salt and pepper. Pour over corn. Sprinkle bread crumbs on top. Place baking dish in large pan, set on middle oven rack; pour hot water into pan to come halfway up baking dish (this keeps corn mixture from curdling). Bake uncovered at 350° for 1 to 1¼ hours or until mixture is bubbly and topping lightly brown. Serve hot. Serves 4

Celery Water Chestnut Casserole

4 cups celery, 1 inch slices
1 (5 ounce) can water
    chestnuts, drained and
    sliced
1 (10 ounce) can cream of
    chicken soup
¼ cup pimientos, diced
¼ cup soft bread crumbs
¼ cup almonds, toasted and
    slivered
2 tablespoons margarine,
    melted

Cook celery in boiling salted water until crisp-tender, about 8 minutes. Drain, mix celery with water chestnuts, soup and pimientos. Pour in greased 1 quart casserole. Toss crumbs, almonds and margarine together, sprinkle over top. Bake at 350° for 35 minutes. Serve hot. Serves 6

A word spoken pleasantly is a large spot of sunshine on a sad heart. Therefore, "Give others the sunshine, tell Jesus the rest."

Layered Potato Casserole

4 medium potatoes, sliced
½ head cabbage, sliced
1½ cups apple, diced
1 medium onion, sliced
Salt and pepper
3 tablespoons margarine
1 cup whipping cream
½ cup Parmesan cheese
¾ cup bread crumbs

Grease 3 quart casserole. Layer potatoes on bottom, then cabbage, apple and onion. Dot with margarine dabs on top; pour whipping cream over ingredients. Bake 1 to 1½ hours at 350°, covered. Uncover and top with Parmesan cheese and bread crumbs; brown an additional 10 to 15 minutes. This is such a good dish - different with cabbage and apples.

Hobo Potatoes

2 cups potatoes, peeled and
    cubed
1 cup onion, chopped
1 cup carrots, sliced
½ cup celery, sliced
2 tablespoons water
½ teaspoon salt
¼ teaspoon pepper
8 slices bacon, fried and
    crumbled
2 teaspoons margarine

Microwave to Grill Directions:
Heat grill. In 3 quart microwave safe casserole, combine potatoes, onions, carrots, celery and water. Cover with plastic wrap. Microwave on HIGH 5 to 6 minutes or until vegetables are hot and just begin to cook, stirring once. Drain. Stir in salt and pepper. Place potato mixture on 18 x 18 inch square of heavy-duty foil. Top with bacon and dot with margarine. Wrap securely with double fold seal. Immediately place on grill 4 to 6 inches from medium-high coals. Cook, 25 to 30 minutes or until vegetables are tender. These are so good and great to put on the grill when you are grilling steak or chicken. Serves 6

Best Ever Twice-Baked Potatoes

6 large baking potatoes,
   washed
½ cup margarine
1 cup sour cream
4 green onions, chopped
6 slices bacon, fried and
   crumbled
1 teaspoon parsley
1½ cups Cheddar cheese,
   grated
½ teaspoon salt
½ teaspoon pepper
½ teaspoon garlic salt
1 egg

Bake potatoes until done in center. Cut potatoes in half lengthwise. Scoop out pulp and place in bowl. Mash potatoes with margarine, add sour cream, beat until smooth. Add all other ingredients, reserve ½ cup cheese for topping. Spoon mixture into potato shells. Top with cheese and bake at 350° for 20 minutes or until heated thoroughly. *These are our families' favorite baked potatoes. Great with any meat served.* Serves 10 to 12

Broccoli/Cheese Twice-Baked Potatoes

6 medium potatoes
½ cup sour cream
3 tablespoons margarine
½ teaspoon salt
¼ teaspoon pepper
2 green onions, sliced
1½ cups broccoli, cooked
   and chopped
1 cup Cheddar cheese,
   grated and divided
Paprika

Bake potatoes at 350° for 1 to 1½ hours or until soft. Cut a lengthwise slice from the top of potatoes. Scoop out pulp and place in bowl. Mash potatoes; add sour cream, margarine, salt, pepper, onions, broccoli and ¾ cup cheese. Refill potato shells; top with remaining cheese and sprinkle with paprika. Bake at 425° for 20 to 25 minutes or until heated through. Serves 6

Scalloped Potatoes

**6 medium potatoes, scrubbed
  and sliced
1 medium onion, sliced
Whipping cream
Salt and pepper**

Put potatoes and onions in greased casserole dish, add salt and pepper to taste. Add enough whipping cream to potatoes to barely cover. Bake at 350° for 1½ hours or until tender. *Serve these with pinto beans and cornbread for a fabulous meal. These potatoes are great! This is another recipe passed down in our family. It is a "never fail" and the only scalloped potatoes we had as kids growing up.* Serves 6

Parsley Potatoes

**4 large potatoes
1 cup water
3 tablespoons margarine
⅛ teaspoon garlic salt
2 teaspoons dried parsley
¼ teaspoon salt**

Wash potatoes. Slice into ¼ inch slices. In cookie sheet, place sliced potatoes in single layer. Add water. Bake 10 to 12 minutes at 375°. Increase cooking temperature to 450° to brown, cooking 5 to 7 minutes. In small saucepan, melt margarine. Add garlic and cook 2 minutes stirring until golden. Pour over potatoes, add parsley and salt. Toss to coat. Serves 8

You can always count on God to make the "afterward" of difficulties, if rightly overcome, a thousand times richer and fairer than the forward.

Baked Cajun Cabbage

1 large head cabbage
1 cup onion, chopped
1 cup celery, chopped
1 cup bell pepper, chopped

Cheese Sauce
½ cup margarine
4 tablespoons flour
1½ cups milk
Salt
Cayenne pepper to taste
½ pound Cheddar cheese,
    grated

Topping
1 cup green onions, chopped
¼ cup seasoned bread
    crumbs

Remove outer leaves from cabbage. Cut into bite-size sections, removing heart. Boil about 10 minutes, uncovered, until crisp-tender. Drain; set aside. In separate saucepan, combine margarine and flour, blending well over medium heat. Add onions, celery, pepper, salt and cayenne pepper. Sauté for 10 minutes. Add milk, blending well over low heat until creamy. Add cheese; stir until smooth. Place cabbage in 2 quart casserole; top with seasoned cheese sauce. Sprinkle with green onions and bread crumbs. Bake at 350° for 30 minutes. Serves 6

Sauerkraut Casserole

1 pound mild Italian sausage
    links, cut into 1-inch
    slices
1 large onion, chopped
2 apples, peeled and
    quartered
1 (27 ounce) can sauerkraut,
    undrained
1 cup water
½ cup brown sugar
2 teaspoons caraway seed

In skillet, cook sausage and onion until sausage is brown and onion is tender; drain. Stir in apples, sauerkraut, water, brown sugar and caraway seed. Transfer to a 2½ quart baking dish. Cover and bake at 350° for 1 hour. Serves 6

Tangy Mustard Cauliflower

Microwave
1 medium head cauliflower,
    cut into florets
2 tablespoons water
½ cup mayonnaise
1 teaspoon onion, chopped
1 teaspoon prepared mustard
½ cup cheese, grated

Combine onion, mayonnaise and mustard. Place cauliflower in 1½ quart casserole dish. Add water and cover with glass lid or plastic wrap. Microwave high power 8 to 9 minutes or until crisp-tender. Spoon mustard sauce on top of cauliflower. Sprinkle with cheese. Put in microwave on low to melt cheese. Let stand 2 minutes before serving. Serves 6

Meats

Beef & Veggies Casserole

1 pound ground beef
1 medium onion, chopped
4½ teaspoons chili powder
1 teaspoon oregano
½ teaspoon salt
1 (16 ounce) can corn,
    drained
1 (16 ounce) can tomatoes,
    chopped
1 (15 ounce) can kidney
    beans
1 cup tortilla chips, crushed
3 ounces Monterey Jack
    cheese, grated

Brown beef and onions. Drain. Add all seasonings. Add tomatoes with liquid, corn, beans and heat over high heat to boiling. Reduce heat and simmer 10 minutes. Put beef mixture into 2 quart casserole dish, sprinkle cheese on meat, top with chips. Bake at 350° uncovered for 20 minutes.

Mexican Fiesta

Meat Sauce
4 pounds ground beef
3 onions, chopped
½ teaspoon garlic salt
4 teaspoons chili powder
1 (15 ounce) can tomato
    sauce
1 (6 ounce) can tomato paste
1 (23 ounce) can ranch style
    beans

Layers
Corn chips, crushed
Rice, cooked
Meat sauce
Lettuce, shredded
Tomatoes, chopped
Cheese, grated
Onion, chopped
Ripe olives, chopped
Salsa
Coconut, flaked
Pecans, chopped

Combine all Meat Sauce ingredients. Simmer for 2 hours.

To serve, stack the layering ingredients on top of each other.

The coconut and pecans add a very unique flavor. This is a fun meal when you have a large bunch to feed. Serves 25

Tamale Pie

2 onions, chopped
2 cloves garlic, minced
1 green bell pepper, chopped
1 pound ground beef
1 tablespoon chili powder
½ teaspoon cumin
1 (15 ounce) can tomato
    sauce
1 (12 ounce) can corn,
    drained
1 (3½ ounce) can black
    olives, sliced and drained
Salt
Pepper
1½ cups Cheddar cheese,
    grated

Crust
¾ cup cornmeal, white or
    yellow
½ teaspoon salt
2 cups water
2 tablespoons margarine
2 eggs

Brown meat, onions, garlic and pepper together. Add seasonings and stir in tomato sauce, corn, and olives. Simmer 30 minutes and remove from heat. Let mixture cool slightly. Place half the mixture in casserole and add half the cheese; repeat layers. (A 1½ quart greased baking dish should be sufficient.) Stir cornmeal and salt into water in saucepan. Cook, stirring until mixture is thickened. Stir in margarine. Beat in eggs. Top casserole with the cornmeal crust and bake 40 minutes at 375°. Serves 6

Hamburger Cream Cheese Casserole

1 pound ground beef
1 medium onion, chopped
1 (8 ounce) package cream
    cheese
1 (11 ounce) can cream of
    mushroom soup
1½ cups corn
Biscuits (homemade or
    canned)

Brown hamburger and onion. Drain. Mix in cream cheese, soup and corn. Pour into greased 2 quart casserole dish. Add biscuits on top and bake at 375° for 25 minutes. Serve with a salad for an excellent quick meal. Serves 6

Barbecue Brisket

5 to 6 pounds brisket
1 (4 ounce) bottle liquid
  smoke
1 teaspoon celery salt
1 teaspoon garlic salt
Salt
Pepper
2 tablespoons
  Worcestershire sauce
1 onion, thinly sliced

Barbecue Sauce
1 cup catsup
1 cup brown sugar
½ cup wine vinegar
1 cup onion, chopped
4 tablespoons lemon juice
1 teaspoon ground black
  pepper
2 (4 ounce) jars plum baby
  food

Marinate brisket in liquid smoke several hours or overnight. Sprinkle with celery salt, garlic salt, salt, pepper and Worcestershire sauce. Put thinly sliced onions over top. Bake covered in shallow baking dish at 300° for 4 to 5 hours. Last hour uncover and top with Barbecue Sauce. Slice diagonally. Serves 8

For sauce, combine all ingredients and bring to a boil, stirring constantly. Continue to simmer for 7 minutes. Excellent over the brisket, hamburgers, roast beef and little smokies.

Sage Meatballs

2 pounds ground beef
1 teaspoon sage
1 medium onion, chopped
½ teaspoon salt
½ teaspoon pepper
1 egg
1 (11 ounce) can cream of
  mushroom soup
1 (11 ounce) can cream of
  celery soup

Mix beef, sage, onion, salt, pepper and egg together and form into small balls and brown in skillet. Place meatballs in 2-quart greased casserole dish. Pour soups over meatballs. Bake covered at 325° for 1 hour. Serve over rice or noodles. *These meatballs are so good served with salad and bread for a wonderful meal.* Serves 8

Remember, a smile adds to your face value.

Ground Beef Casserole

1½ pounds ground beef
1 onion, chopped
1 (16 ounce) can chili
1 cup ripe olives, sliced
1 cup mushrooms, sliced
1½ cups Cheddar cheese, grated
2 cups corn chips, crushed

Brown beef and onions. Drain. Add chili, olives and mushrooms. Pour into a 2 quart greased casserole dish. Sprinkle with cheese and top with crushed corn chips. Bake at 350° for 30 minutes or until cheese bubbles. Serve with a salad. Serves 8

Beef Stroganoff

1½ pounds ground beef
1 to 2 cloves garlic, minced
1 medium onion, chopped
1 cup mushrooms, sliced
1 (11 ounce) can cream of mushroom soup
1 (11 ounce) can cream of chicken soup
1 cup sour cream

Brown beef, garlic and onions. Drain; add mushrooms and soups. Simmer 30 to 45 minutes. Just before serving, stir in sour cream. Serve over rice or noodles. (This recipe can also be made with round steak cut into small pieces. Follow same directions.) Serves 6

Spaghetti Skillet Dinner

1½ pounds ground beef
¼ cup green bell pepper, chopped
⅓ cup onion, chopped
½ cup celery, chopped
½ cup carrots, sliced
2 cups stewed tomatoes
1½ teaspoons salt
¼ teaspoon pepper
2 cups corn, with liquid
⅔ cup mushrooms, sliced
4 ounces spaghetti, broken in thirds

Brown beef, pepper, and onions. Add celery, carrots, corn, mushrooms and spaghetti pieces. Pour tomatoes over all and sprinkle with seasonings. Cover and simmer for 30 minutes or until spaghetti is done. *This is so easy and my kids loved this when they were "little".* Serves 8

Mexican Lasagna

1 pound ground beef
1 (16 ounce) can refried
   beans
2 teaspoons oregano
1 teaspoon cumin
¾ teaspoon garlic powder
12 uncooked lasagna
   noodles
2½ cups water
2½ cups salsa
2 cups sour cream
¾ cup green onions, sliced
½ cup black olives, drained
   and sliced
1 cup Monterey Jack cheese,
   grated

Combine beef, beans, oregano, cumin and garlic powder. Place four of the uncooked lasagna noodles in bottom of greased 9 x 13 inch baking pan. Spread half the beef mixture over noodles. Top with four more noodles and remaining beef mixture. Cover with remaining noodles. Combine water and salsa. Pour over all. Cover tightly with foil. Bake at 350° for 1½ hours or until noodles are tender. Combine sour cream, onions and olives. Spoon over casserole; top with cheese and bake uncovered until cheese is melted, about 5 minutes. Serves 8

Reunion Casserole

1 pound ground beef
½ pound sausage
1 cup onions, chopped
2 cups Cheddar cheese,
   grated and divided
1 green bell pepper, chopped
1 (12 ounce) can corn,
   drained
1 (11 ounce) can tomato soup
1 (8 ounce) can tomato sauce
⅓ cup green olives, sliced
1 clove garlic, minced
½ teaspoon salt
8 ounces wide noodles,
   cooked and drained

Brown beef, onions, and peppers. Mix all ingredients except 1 cup cheese. Pour into greased 9 x 13 inch pan and top with 1 cup cheese. Bake at 350° for 30 minutes. This is a great dish for reunions and large gatherings. Serves 10

Mexican Casserole

2 pounds ground beef
1 medium onion, chopped
1 pound Velveeta cheese,
  cubed
1 (11 ounce) can cream of
  chicken soup
1 (11 ounce) can cream of
  mushroom soup
1 (15 ounce) can mild
  enchilada sauce
1 (4 ounce) can green chilies
1 package (10) corn tortillas,
  cut in fourths

Brown beef and onions. Drain. Add cheese and stir until melted. Mix in soups, enchilada sauce and chilies. Stir in tortillas. Pour in greased 2 quart casserole dish. Bake at 350° for 25 minutes. This is a good casserole served with a salad. Makes a super make-ahead meal. Serves 8

Layered Cheese and Beef Casserole

4 cups uncooked medium
  egg noodles
1 pound ground beef
¾ cup onion, chopped
2 (8 ounce) cans tomato
  sauce
1 teaspoon salt
½ teaspoon garlic powder
¼ teaspoon pepper
1 cup cottage cheese
1 (8 ounce) package cream
  cheese, softened
⅓ cup green onions, sliced
¼ cup green bell pepper,
  chopped
½ cup Parmesan cheese

Cook noodles to desired doneness as directed on package; drain. In medium skillet brown beef and ¾ cup onions; drain. Add tomato sauce, salt, garlic powder and pepper; mix well. Reduce heat; simmer 15 minutes. In medium bowl, combine cottage cheese, cream cheese, green onions, pepper and ½ cup Parmesan cheese; mix well. In ungreased 9 x 13 inch baking dish, layer half each of cooked noodles, meat sauce and cheese mixture; repeat layers. Sprinkle additional Parmesan cheese over top. Bake at 350° for 30 to 35 minutes or until thoroughly heated. Serve this casserole with a green veggie or salad for a complete meal. Serves 8

Pizza Loaf

1 package pizza dough
1 cup pizza sauce or
   spaghetti sauce
1 pound ground beef
¼ cup onion, chopped
1 (4 ounce) can mushrooms,
   drained
2 tablespoons flour
1 tablespoon sweet pepper
   flakes
1 teaspoon paprika
¼ teaspoon oregano
⅛ teaspoon pepper
½ cup black olives, chopped
1 cup Cheddar cheese,
   grated
Milk
Sesame seeds

Sauce
1 (11 ounce) can tomato soup
1 cup Cheddar cheese,
   grated
½ teaspoon dry mustard
1 teaspoon Worcestershire
   sauce

Combine pizza sauce, beef, onions, mushrooms, flour, sweet pepper flakes, paprika, oregano and pepper in skillet. Cook over medium heat 15 minutes. Remove from heat and stir in olives. Cool for 10 minutes. Put pizza dough on 14 x 11 inch rectangle pan. Place meat mixture down center third of dough to within 2 inches of ends. Sprinkle with Cheddar cheese. Make diagonal cuts 2 inches apart, on each side of rectangle just to edge of filling. Fold ends over filling. Then fold strips over filling alternating sides and crossing in center. Brush with milk and sprinkle with sesame seeds. Bake at 400° for 15 to 20 minutes or until golden brown. Serve as is or with sauce.

Combine tomato soup, cheese, dry mustard and Worcestershire sauce in saucepan. Heat over low heat until cheese is melted and mixture is smooth. This is another recipe that you can make a salad with and call it lunch or supper. Serve hot.

Winning is an inside job.

Meat and Potato Casserole

1 pound ground beef
4 medium potatoes, sliced
2 tablespoons flour
¼ teaspoon salt
¼ teaspoon pepper
1 (26 ounce) can family-size
    vegetable soup
1 cup Cheddar cheese,
    grated

Brown beef in large skillet, drain. In ungreased 2 quart baking dish, evenly layer potato slices. In small bowl, combine flour, salt and pepper. Sprinkle over potato slices. Spoon ground beef over potatoes; spoon vegetable soup evenly over top. Cover with foil. Bake at 350° for 1 hour or until potatoes are tender. Uncover; sprinkle with cheese. Bake an additional 5 minutes. Serves 4

Chili Relleno Bake

½ pound ground beef
½ pound pork sausage
    (chorizo is great)
1 cup onion, chopped
2 cloves garlic, minced
2 (4 ounces) cans whole
    green chilies, drained and
    seeded
2 cups Cheddar cheese,
    grated, divided
4 eggs
¼ cup flour
1½ cups milk
½ teaspoon salt
Tabasco

In large skillet, crumble together beef, sausage, onion and garlic. Cook over medium heat, stirring until meat is browned. Drain. Line 9 x 9 inch baking dish with half of the chilies; top with 1½ cups of cheese. Add meat mixture, top with remaining chilies; set aside. Beat together eggs and flour until smooth; add milk, salt and Tabasco. Blend well. Pour egg mixture over casserole. Bake, uncovered at 350° for 40 minutes or until knife inserted comes out clean. Sprinkle remaining ½ cup cheese on top. Let stand 5 minutes before serving. Serves 4

Don't just achieve your goals, strive to exceed your goals.

Flank Steak Béarnaise

1 (8 ounce) package cream
   cheese, cubed
¼ cup milk
1 tablespoon green onion,
   sliced
½ teaspoon tarragon,
   crushed
2 egg yolks, beaten
2 tablespoons dry white wine
1 tablespoon lemon juice
1 (1½ pounds) flank steak

In saucepan, combine cream cheese, milk, green onions and tarragon; stir over low heat until cream cheese is melted. Stir small amount of hot cream cheese mixture into egg yolks; return to hot mixture. Stir in wine and juice. Cook, stirring constantly, over low heat 1 minute or until thickened. Score steak on both sides. Place on rack of broiler pan (or grill). Broil on both sides to desired doneness. With knife slanted, carve steak across grain into thin slices. Serve with cream cheese mixture. Serves 6

Prime Rib

Standing Rib Roast - any size
   (let roast come to room
   temperature)
Salt
Pepper
Garlic powder
Thyme (optional)
Rosemary (optional)

Six hours before meal time, heat oven to 400°. Season roast. Place in a shallow roasting pan, uncovered. Cook for 1 hour, then turn oven off - DO NOT OPEN OVEN! Forty minutes before serving, turn oven on to 375° to finish cooking. *This is a great way to cook standing rib roast so it is crusty and brown on the outside and medium rare in the center. Remove roast from oven and let stand 5 minutes before slicing. The aroma makes everyone anxious for dinner. My family loves this served with twice baked potatoes,* (Refer to index) *salad and rolls.*

Oriental Pork Stew

1 pound boneless pork, cut into 1 inch cubes
½ cup onion, chopped
1 clove garlic, minced
2 tablespoons oil
2 cups water
1 beef flavored bouillon cube
¼ cup soy sauce
1 cup celery, sliced
1 red or green bell pepper, sliced
1 cup frozen green beans
1 (8 ounce) can sliced water chestnuts, drained
2 cups mushrooms, sliced
½ cup water
3 tablespoons cornstarch
Crisp chow mein noodles

In large saucepan or Dutch oven, sauté meat, onion, and garlic in oil until meat is brown. Stir in 2 cups water, bouillon and soy sauce. Bring to a boil; reduce heat. Cover and simmer 30 minutes or until pork is tender. Add celery, red pepper, green beans, water chestnuts and mushrooms. Bring to boil. Reduce heat. Cover; simmer an additional 5 to 10 minutes or until vegetables are crisp-tender. Mix ½ cup water and cornstarch. Stir into vegetable mixture; cook until thickened. Serve with crisp chow mein noodles or rice. Serves 4

Pork Chop and Chilies Casserole

1 tablespoon oil
4 pork chops
1 medium onion, chopped
1 (4 ounce) can green chilies, chopped
½ cup celery, chopped
1½ cups uncooked instant rice
1 (11 ounce) can cream of mushroom soup
1 soup can water
3 tablespoons soy sauce

In skillet, heat oil over medium-high heat. Brown pork chops on both sides. Remove and set aside. In same skillet, sauté onions, chilies, and celery until tender. Stir in rice; sauté until lightly browned. Add all remaining ingredients; blend well. Place in greased 2 quart casserole. Top with pork chops. Cover and bake at 350° for about 30 minutes or until rice is tender. Serves 4

Sweet and Sour Pork

3½ pounds lean spare ribs
   (4 to 5 pork chops)
½ onion, chopped
¼ cup green bell pepper,
   chopped
⅓ cup brown sugar
½ cup vinegar
1 tablespoon soy sauce
1 cup pineapple juice
½ teaspoon salt
⅛ teaspoon pepper
1 tablespoon cornstarch
1 cup water
1 cup pineapple chunks,
   drained

Brown meat; set aside. Brown onions and peppers in same skillet. Add brown sugar, vinegar, soy sauce, pineapple juice, salt, pepper and meat. Cover and simmer for 2 hours. Remove meat. Mix cornstarch and water, add to sauce. Cook until thickened. Place meat in 9 x 13 inch baking dish, pour sauce over meat and bake at 350° for 30 minutes. Add pineapple chunks last five minutes. This is a wonderful way to fix pork. Serve with rice. Serves 4

Apricot-Glazed Country Ribs

3 to 4 pounds country-style
   pork ribs
1 small onion, sliced

Glaze
½ cup apricot preserves
2 tablespoons lemon juice
1 teaspoon ginger
2 teaspoons soy sauce
1 clove garlic, minced

Microwave-to-grill directions: Heat grill. Place ribs in a 2 quart microwave-safe dish, keeping thickest portions to outside edge of dish. Add sliced onions. Cover with plastic wrap. Microwave on HIGH for 12 to 15 minutes or until ribs are no longer pink, rearranging and turning ribs over halfway through cooking; drain. Meanwhile, in small bowl combine all glaze ingredients; blend well. Immediately place ribs on gas grill over medium heat or on charcoal grill 4 to 6 inches from medium coals. Cook 8 to 12 minutes; turn. Cook an additional 8 to 12 minutes or until ribs are tender, brushing with glaze several times during last 8 minutes. Serves 5 to 6

Cook's Tips

Wood Chips to Flavor Barbecued Foods

- Fruit Woods: Delicate and sweet. Best for poultry, seafood and pork.

- Grapevine: Delicate and sweet. Best for delicate fish or poultry.

- Hickory: Popular, intense and smoky. Best for robust food, such as ribs, poultry and beef.

- Mesquite: Light, clean and woody. Best for meats compatible with strong flavor such as beef, chicken and swordfish.

- Nut Woods: Delicate and sweet. Best for poultry and dark fish such as tuna.

- Oak: Mellow and fresh. Best for meats compatible with strong flavor such as steak, pork, chicken and salmon.

Tucsan Pork and Pasta

2 cups uncooked penne
   (medium pasta tubes)
2 tablespoons olive oil
¾ to 1 pound pork
   tenderloins, cut into
   ¼ inch slices
½ cup green onions, sliced
2 cloves garlic, minced
2 cups Italian plum tomatoes,
   sliced
¼ cup dry white wine
½ teaspoon dried basil
¼ teaspoon salt
¼ teaspoon pepper

Cook penne to desired doneness as directed on package. Drain; keep warm. Meanwhile, heat oil in large skillet. Add pork, onions and garlic; cook 8 to 10 minutes or until pork is browned on both sides, stirring frequently. Stir in tomatoes, wine, basil, salt and pepper. Bring to a boil. Reduce heat; simmer 3 to 4 minutes or until pork is no longer pink and sauce is slightly thickened, stirring frequently. To serve, spoon pork mixture over cooked penne. Serves 3 to 4

Sesame Pork and Mushroom Pasta

1 (7 ounce) package
  uncooked vermicelli
2 tablespoons margarine
2 teaspoons sesame oil
1 pound pork tenderloin,
  cut into ¼ inch slices
3 to 4 thin slices red onion,
  cut in half
1 tablespoon sesame seeds
2 cloves garlic, minced
6 ounces fresh pea pods,
  trimmed
1 cup mushrooms, sliced
¼ cup Parmesan cheese,
  grated

Cook vermicelli to desired doneness as directed on package; drain. Keep warm. Heat margarine and oil in large skillet over medium-high heat. Add pork, onion, sesame seeds and garlic. Cook and stir until pork is no longer pink, about 5 to 6 minutes. Add pea pods; cook and stir 2 to 3 minutes or until crisp-tender. Stir in mushrooms. Serve pork and vegetable mixture over hot vermicelli. Sprinkle with Parmesan cheese. This is full of flavor without the heavy sauces. Serves 4

Bratwurst-Apple Skillet

4 cooked bratwurst
½ cup red bell pepper,
  chopped
½ cup beer or nonalcoholic
  beer
1 to 2 teaspoons caraway
  seed
1 (16 ounce) can sauerkraut,
  drained
1 large cooking apple, cored,
  sliced

Brown bratwurst in medium skillet over medium-high heat, turning occasionally. In medium bowl, combine all remaining ingredients; add to skillet. Reduce heat; cover and simmer 8 to 12 minutes or until apples are tender, stirring occasionally. Serves 4

Seasoning Tips for Grilling

Since salt extracts the natural juices from meats during grilling, add it after grilling is completed.

Apple Pork Chops

1⅓ cups water
2 tablespoons margarine
2 tablespoons green onions,
    sliced
¼ teaspoon salt
½ cup milk
1½ cups mashed potato
    flakes
¼ cup Cheddar cheese,
    grated
4 pork chops
1 tablespoon margarine
1 tablespoon flour
1 tablespoon brown sugar
1 cup unsweetened apple
    juice or cider
1 large apple, cored, cut into
    4 rings
Cinnamon

In medium saucepan, heat water, 2 tablespoons margarine, green onions and salt to rolling boil; remove from heat. Add milk and potato flakes; stir to desired consistency. Stir in cheese. In large skillet, brown pork chops in 1 tablespoon margarine. Place pork chops in 2 quart baking dish. Stir flour and brown sugar into meat drippings in skillet to make thick paste. Gradually add apple juice; cook until mixture thickens, stirring constantly. Place 1 apple ring on each chop; sprinkle with cinnamon. Pour apple juice mixture over pork chops. Mound ¼ potatoes on top of each apple ring. Bake at 350° for 40 to 50 minutes or until pork chops are tender. This is a favorite of my family. Serves 4

Grilled Pork Tenderloin

2 (1 pound each) pork
    tenderloins
1 (8 ounce) bottle low-fat,
    low-cal Italian dressing

Place tenderloins in bowl. Pour dressing over. Cover and refrigerate for 6 to 8 hours or overnight. Grill over hot coals for 15 to 20 minutes or until done. Slice and serve immediately. Serves 6

Plum and Apple Pork Tenderloin

1 teaspoon oil
1 pound pork tenderloins,
   cut into ½ inch slices
¼ teaspoon salt
⅛ teaspoon pepper
2 ripe plums, pitted, sliced
1 large apple, unpeeled,
   sliced
½ cup apple cider or juice
2 tablespoons brown sugar
2 teaspoons cornstarch
1 tablespoon water

Heat oil in large skillet. Add pork; sprinkle with salt and pepper. Cook 5 to 7 minutes or until pork is tender and no longer pink. Add plums, apple and apple cider. Cover; simmer 10 minutes or until fruit is tender. In small bowl, combine remaining ingredients; add to skillet. Cook over medium heat until mixture is thickened and bubbly, stirring constantly; boil 1 minute. You can use any kind of plums for this recipe. Serve with rice or noodles for a great meal. Serves 4

Mexican Chicken Casserole

1 cooked chicken, boned and
   cubed
1 large onion, chopped
1 package corn tortillas (10)
1 (11 ounce) can cream of
   mushroom soup
1 (11 ounce) can cream of
   chicken soup
1 (11 ounce) can Rotel
   tomatoes
1 cup chicken broth
3 cups Cheddar cheese,
   grated

Cut tortillas in 1 inch squares, put them on bottom of a 9 x 13 inch pan. Sauté onions, add chicken and 2 cups cheese. Mix all liquids with chicken broth, pour over dish. Sprinkle remaining cheese on top. Bake at 350° for 30 to 40 minutes.

Yogurt Grilled Chicken

½ cup plain low-fat yogurt
1 green onion, chopped
1 teaspoon oregano
1 tablespoon olive oil
1 tablespoon wine vinegar
1 teaspoon salt
⅛ teaspoon pepper
4 large boneless, skinless
   chicken breast halves

In large bowl, mix yogurt, green onions, oregano, oil, vinegar, salt and pepper. Add chicken, toss to mix. Marinate 15 minutes, turning chicken once. Heat grill. Place chicken on grill. Grill until fork tender, turning once. Brush with yogurt mixture during grilling. This is great served with mixed veggies and sliced tomatoes. Serves 4

Pasta 'N Chicken in Bread Bowls

5 large hard rolls (about
   3½ inch diameter)
3 tablespoons margarine
¼ cup flour
½ teaspoon basil
¼ teaspoon oregano
¼ teaspoon pepper
1 (11 ounce) can condensed
   chicken broth
1 cup milk
1 tablespoon dry sherry,
   (optional)
1 (16 ounce) package frozen
   vegetables and pasta
2 cups cooked chicken,
   cubed

Scoop out centers of rolls, leaving 1 inch sides. Cover bread bowls; set aside. Melt margarine in large skillet or saucepan. Stir in flour, basil, oregano and pepper until blended. Gradually stir in chicken broth, milk and sherry; cook until thickened, stirring constantly. Add chicken, vegetables and pasta. Bring to boil. Reduce heat to low; cover and simmer 5 to 8 minutes or until vegetables are tender. Place bread bowls on individual serving plates; fill with chicken mixture. This will be a hearty family favorite. Serves 5

Lemon Herb Marinated Chicken

2 tablespoons oil
1 tablespoon lemon juice
½ teaspoon basil
½ teaspoon tarragon
½ teaspoon salt
¼ teaspoon pepper
1 pound boneless, skinless
    chicken breast halves

In cup, mix first 5 ingredients; pour over chicken. Cover; let stand at room temperature no longer than 30 minutes, turning once. Grill 10 minutes or until thoroughly cooked, turning once. *These are so easy to throw on the grill for a quick meal.* Serves 4

Chicken Crescent Almondine

1 (11 ounce) can cream of
    chicken soup
⅔ cup mayonnaise
½ cup sour cream
2 tablespoons onion,
    chopped
3 cups cooked chicken,
    cubed
1 (6 ounce) can water
    chestnuts, sliced and
    drained
1 cup mushrooms, sliced
½ cup celery, chopped
1 (8 ounce) can crescent
    dinner rolls
⅔ cup Swiss or American
    cheese, grated
2 tablespoons margarine,
    melted
½ cup almonds, slivered

In large saucepan, combine soup, mayonnaise, sour cream and onions. Stir in chicken, water chestnuts, mushrooms and celery; cook until hot and bubbly. Pour in 9 x 13 inch baking dish. Unroll crescent rolls and cover meat mixture. Combine cheese and almonds and sprinkle over dough. Drizzle with margarine. Bake at 375° for 20 to 25 minutes.

A change in your attitude can change your life.

Crab and Spinach-Stuffed Chicken Breasts

4 large boneless, skinless
    chicken breast halves

Sauce
½ cup light sour cream
½ cup reduced-calorie
    mayonnaise
2 tablespoons lowfat milk
2 teaspoon Dijon mustard

Stuffing
1 (9 ounce) package frozen
    spinach, thawed,
    squeezed to drain
¼ cup green onions, chopped
2 tablespoons green bell
    pepper, chopped
2 tablespoons fresh parsley,
    chopped
2 tablespoons pine nuts,
    toasted
1 (6 ounce) can crabmeat,
    drained, rinsed and flaked
¼ teaspoon salt
Dash pepper

Coating
¼ cup water or brandy
3 tablespoons margarine,
    melted
½ cup dry bread crumbs
½ teaspoon paprika
2 (10 ounce) packages frozen
    rice and broccoli

Combine sour cream, mayonnaise, milk and mustard; blend well and set aside. Place 1 chicken breast half between 2 pieces of plastic wrap or waxed paper. Working from center, gently pound chicken with rolling pin or flat side of meat mallet until ¼ inch thick. Repeat with remaining chicken breasts. In medium bowl, combine spinach, green onions, green pepper, parsley, pine nuts, crabmeat and 3 tablespoons of the sauce; mix well. Sprinkle chicken breasts with salt and pepper. Place about ½ cup spinach mixture on each chicken breast. Bring one end of breast over spinach mixture. Fold in sides; roll up jelly-roll fashion. In shallow dish, combine butter and water or brandy. In another shallow dish, combine bread crumbs and paprika. Dip each chicken roll in margarine mixture; coat with crumb mixture. Arrange chicken, seam side down in 1½ quart baking dish. Cover and bake at 375° for 30 to 40 minutes or until chicken is no longer pink. Meanwhile, prepare frozen rice and broccoli according to package directions. Heat remaining sauce. To serve, place chicken on prepared rice; spoon sauce over chicken. Pass remaining sauce. This is a super dish for entertaining and you can also do it in the microwave. Serves 4

Chicken Enchilada Casserole

10 corn tortillas, torn in
    pieces
6 cups cooked chicken,
    cubed
1 medium onion, chopped
1 green or red bell pepper,
    chopped
1 (11 ounce) can cream of
    mushroom soup
1 (11 ounce) can cream of
    chicken soup
1 cup salsa
1 cup black olives, chopped
1 (4 ounce) can green chilies,
    diced
¾ cup chicken broth
2 cups Cheddar cheese,
    grated
1 cup tortilla chips, crushed

Sauté onions and peppers until tender. Reserve ½ cup of cheese and tortilla chips. Mix all other ingredients together. Pour into a greased 9 x 13 inch baking dish. Top with remaining cheese and tortilla chips. Bake at 350° for 30 to 40 minutes. Serves 8

Baked Chicken Breasts Supreme

1½ cups plain yogurt
¼ cup lemon juice
½ teaspoon Worcestershire
    sauce
½ teaspoon celery seed
½ teaspoon paprika
1 clove garlic, minced
½ teaspoon salt
¼ teaspoon pepper
8 boneless, skinless chicken
    breast halves
2 cups fine dry bread crumbs

In large bowl, combine first eight ingredients. Place chicken in mixture and turn to coat. Cover and marinate 2 hours in refrigerator. Remove chicken from marinade; coat each piece with crumbs. Arrange on shallow baking pan. Bake uncovered at 350° for 45 minutes of until juices run clear. This is great for a busy day. Make ahead and bake just before serving. Leftovers make great sandwiches. Serves 8

Margarita Chicken Breasts

4 boneless, skinless chicken breast halves, rinsed and dried
¼ cup tequila
2 tablespoons lime juice, fresh
1 tablespoon brown sugar
1 teaspoon fresh cilantro leaves, minced
3 cloves garlic, minced
3 tablespoons flour
⅛ teaspoon oregano
¼ teaspoon cumin
1 teaspoon salt
2 tablespoons oil
½ red onion, thinly sliced
½ red sweet bell pepper, cut in rings
4 large fresh mushrooms, sliced

Pound chicken breasts with meat mallet to flatten and tenderize. In bowl, combine tequila, lime juice, brown sugar, cilantro and garlic. Add chicken. Cover and refrigerate ½ hour, turning once. Transfer chicken to plate, reserving marinade. On separate plate, thoroughly combine flour, oregano, cumin and salt. Dredge chicken in flour mixture, reserving some for dredging mushrooms. In medium skillet, heat oil very hot, but not smoking. Sauté chicken quickly, turning once until browned and almost done. Transfer chicken to oven-to-table dish suitable for placing under broiler. Pour reserved marinade into sauté skillet and bring to boil while scraping up browned pan essences with wooden spoon. Reduce heat to medium and cook till sauce reduces. Taste to correct seasoning, then add chicken, onion and peppers. Dredge mushrooms in remaining flour mixture and add to pan, spooning sauce over all while cooking 5 minutes. Transfer skillet contents to broiling dish and place under preheated broiler just until chicken is glazed and sauce bubbles. Serve piping hot with Spanish rice; black beans flavored with garlic, cumin and cilantro and cornbread.

Chicken Roll-Ups

**4 boneless, skinless chicken
   breasts halves
1 cup dried apricots,
   chopped
1 tablespoon onion flakes
¼ teaspoon garlic salt
Pepper
1 to 2 tablespoons margarine,
   melted**

With meat mallet pound each chicken breast to ¼ inch thickness. Sprinkle with onion flakes and garlic salt. Put ¼ cup apricots on each breast. Roll up chicken breasts and secure with toothpicks. Place in baking dish and brush with melted margarine. Bake at 350° until juices run clear. (Do not cover while baking.) To serve, slice 1 inch thick. Serve with veggies and rice. This are one of my family's favorite chicken dishes. Serves 4

Sassy Sauce for Poultry

**1 small jar Russian dressing
½ cup apricot preserves
1 package dry onion soup**

Mix together and pour over chicken before baking. Can also be cooked and served as sauce for chicken or turkey.

Apricot-Mustard Glaze

**½ cup dried apricots
1 cup orange juice
2 tablespoons Dijon mustard
1 teaspoon honey**

In small saucepan combine apricots and orange juice. Simmer 10 minutes. Puree mixture in food processor or blender. Transfer to small mixing bowl and stir in mustard and honey. Refrigerate until ready to use. This glaze is great on ham, chicken, pork or hamburgers. Makes about ¾ cup

Grilled Fillets of Fish

Sauce
1½ cups tomato, chopped
1 avocado, chopped
¼ cup green onions, chopped
1 (4 ounce) can green chiles, diced
2 tablespoons white wine vinegar
1 tablespoon oil
½ teaspoon salt
1 tablespoon fresh cilantro, chopped

Fish
1½ pounds fresh or frozen cod, halibut or other firm fish, thawed
1 to 2 tablespoons oil

In medium bowl, combine all sauce ingredients; mix well. Cover and refrigerate. When ready to barbecue, oil grill rack. Place fish on grill over medium heat. Brush fish lightly with 1 tablespoon oil. Cook 12 to 15 minutes or until fish flakes easily with fork, turning once and brushing lightly with remaining oil. To serve, top with sauce. Serves 6

Fish Fillets Au Gratin

2 (8 ounce) flounder fillets
1 tablespoon lemon juice
1 teaspoon fresh parsley, chopped
½ teaspoon onion salt
½ teaspoon paprika
¼ teaspoon pepper
½ cup American cheese, grated

Place frozen fish fillets in ungreased 2 quart baking dish. Sprinkle with lemon juice, parsley, onion salt, paprika and pepper. Bake at 350° for 23 to 28 minutes or until fish flakes easily with fork. Sprinkle cheese over fish. Bake for an additional 1 to 2 minutes or until cheese is melted. Serves 4

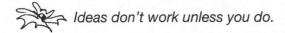

Ideas don't work unless you do.

Grilled Basil Salmon Steaks

Basil Sauce
½ cup packed fresh basil
   leaves
3 tablespoons olive oil
2 tablespoons lemon juice
2 tablespoons honey
½ teaspoon pepper
⅛ teaspoon salt

Steaks
4 (4 to 6 ounce) fresh or
   frozen salmon steaks,
   about 1 inch thick, thawed
1 cup mesquite wood chips,
   optional

In blender or food processor combine all basil sauce ingredients. Process until smooth. Place salmon steaks in 2 quart glass baking dish. Pour sauce over salmon; turn to coat. Cover; refrigerate 30 minutes. Meanwhile, cover wood chips with water, soak 30 minutes. Sprinkle wood chips over rock in grill. Heat grill. When ready to barbecue, oil grill rack. Place salmon on grill over medium-high heat. Cook 10 to 17 minutes or until fish flakes easily with fork, turning once and basting occasionally with sauce. Garnish with lemon slices and a sprig of fresh basil. Serves 4

Grilled Fish Kabobs

½ cup prepared sweet and
   sour sauce
1 tablespoon olive oil
1 pound fresh or frozen
   halibut or haddock, cut
   into 1¼ inch cubes
2 nectarines, cut into eighths
2 small oranges, cut into
   fourths

In medium bowl, combine sweet and sour sauce and oil; mix well. Add fish cubes; stir to coat. Marinate at room temperature for 30 minutes, stirring once. Drain fish, reserving sauce. Alternately thread fish and fruit on 4 metal skewers; brush with sauce. Oil grill rack. Place on grill over medium heat. Cook 8 to 13 minutes or until fish flakes easily with fork, turning and brushing with sauce. Serves 4

Desserts

Rollin' Pin Strawberry Pie

3 egg whites
½ teaspoon baking powder
¾ cup sugar
10 soda crackers, crushed
   fine
½ cup pecans, chopped
2 to 3 pints fresh
   strawberries, sliced
Frozen whipped topping,
   thawed

Spray 9 inch pie pan with non-stick cooking spray. Beat egg whites and baking powder until stiff. Add sugar and continue beating until very stiff. *Fold* in crackers and pecans. Pour into pie pan. Bake at 300° for 50 minutes. Remove from oven; with fork, press crust down. Cool completely. Fill with strawberries. (Add no sugar to strawberries.) Press strawberries down to compact them. Cover with whipped topping. Chill at least 2 hours. *For those who remember, this was the favorite pie at the Rollin' Pin Bakery and Restaurant. It is unlike any strawberry pie you will eat! This was the recipe we had the most requests for at our restaurant.* Serves 6 to 8

Pie Crust

4 cups flour
1 tablespoon sugar
1 teaspoon salt
1 teaspoon baking powder
1½ cups lard
1 egg, slightly beaten
1 teaspoon vinegar
1¼ cups water

Cut lard into dry ingredients. Beat egg with vinegar and water; add to dry mix (not a smooth mix). Can be refrigerated up to 1 week if plastic wrapped. This is not as flaky and good if you substitute shortening for the lard. Makes 3 (9 inch) pie crusts

 23 soda crackers equals 1 cup cracker crumbs.

Meringue

3 egg whites
½ cup sugar
Dash of salt

Beat egg whites and salt until stiff, add sugar and continue beating until stiff peaks form. Spread on hot or warm pie. Seal meringue to edge of crust. Bake at 350° until golden brown.

Pecan Pie

1 cup corn syrup (light or dark)
1 cup brown sugar
¼ teaspoon salt
⅓ cup margarine, melted
1 teaspoon vanilla
3 eggs, slightly beaten
1 cup pecans
1 unbaked pie shell (9 inch)

Combine syrup, sugar, salt, margarine, vanilla and eggs; mix well. Stir in pecans. Pour in pie shell. Bake at 350° for 45 minutes. Serves 6 to 8

Cheesecake Pie

1 (8 ounce) package cream cheese, softened
⅓ cup sugar
2 teaspoons vanilla
3½ cups frozen whipped topping, thawed
1 graham cracker pie crust
Assorted fresh fruit

Beat cheese, sugar and vanilla, until smooth. Fold in whipped topping. Spoon into crust. Chill until set, about 4 hours. Before serving, arrange desired fruit on filling. Any fresh fruit is great on this pie - berries, kiwi, peaches, etc. Use some of each for a pretty and delicious pie. Serves 6 to 8

The very hardships that you are enduring in your life today are given by the Master for the explicit purpose of enabling you to win your crown.

Cherry-Peach Pie

3 cups peaches, peeled and
    sliced
2 cups tart pie cherries
¾ cup sugar
¼ cup cornstarch
1 tablespoon lemon juice
2 tablespoons margarine
Pastry for double-crusted pie
    (9 inch)

In bowl, combine peaches, cherries and sugar. Let stand at room temperature for 1½ hours. Drain fruit, reserving syrup. If necessary, add water to syrup to make 1 cup. In saucepan, combine syrup and cornstarch. Cook and stir until mixture thickens. Remove from heat; stir in lemon juice. Gently fold in drained fruit. Put fruit in pastry lined pie pan. Dot with margarine; put top crust on. Bake in 350° oven for 45 to 50 minutes. *Do not let the fruit combination scare you - this pie is wonderful.* Serves 6 to 8

Sour Cream Raisin Pie

½ cup powdered milk
¾ cup sugar
⅛ teaspoon salt
½ teaspoon cinnamon
Dash of nutmeg
3 eggs, separated
3 tablespoons cornstarch
2 cups water
¾ cup raisins
1 tablespoon lemon juice
1 cup sour cream
Frozen whipped topping,
    thawed
1 (9 inch) baked pie shell

Mix milk, sugar, salt, cinnamon, nutmeg, and cornstarch in microwave safe dish. Add egg yolks and a little water; mix until smooth. Add remaining water; mix again. Put in microwave for 2 minutes on high. Remove and stir well. Return to microwave for 2 more minutes on high. Remove and stir again. Return to microwave for 1 to 2 minutes on high. Remove and stir in raisins and lemon juice. Let cool to room temperature. Stir in sour cream. Put in pie shell, top with whipped topping. This pie is quick and easy by making it in microwave. Serves 6 to 8

Lemon Pie

1 cup sugar
2 cups water
⅓ cup cornstarch
3 eggs, separated
⅓ cup lemon juice
2 tablespoons margarine
1 baked pie shell (9 inch)

Mix sugar and cornstarch; add egg yolks and water in microwave safe dish. Mix until smooth. Put in microwave for 2 minutes on high. Remove and stir well. Return to microwave for 2 more minutes on high. Remove and stir again. Return to microwave again for 1 to 2 minutes on high. (If this is too thick, add water for desired consistency.) Stir in lemon juice and margarine. Put in pie shell; top with meringue. (Refer to Meringue) Serves 6 to 8

Coconut Cream Pie

½ cup powdered milk
½ cup sugar
Pinch of salt
¼ cup cornstarch
3 egg yolks
1½ to 2 cups water
1 teaspoon vanilla
2 to 3 tablespoons margarine
¾ cup flaked coconut
1 baked pie shell (9 inch)

Mix powdered milk, sugar and cornstarch; add egg yolks and water in microwave safe dish. Mix until smooth. Put in microwave for 2 minutes on high. Remove and stir well. Return to microwave for 2 more minutes on high. Remove and stir again. Return to microwave again for 1 to 2 minutes on high. (If this is too thick, add water for desired consistency.) Stir in margarine and vanilla. Put in pie shell; top with meringue and sprinkle with flaked coconut. (Refer to Meringue) Serves 6 to 8

Chocolate Cream Pie

½ cup powdered milk
1 cup sugar
Pinch of salt
¼ cup cornstarch
3 egg yolks
1½ to 2 cups water
¾ cup chocolate chips
1 teaspoon vanilla
2 to 3 tablespoons margarine
1 (9 inch) baked pie shell

Mix powdered milk, sugar and cornstarch; add egg yolks and water in microwave safe dish. Mix until smooth. Add chocolate chips and stir. Put in microwave for 2 minutes on high. Remove and stir well. Return to microwave for 2 more minutes on high. Remove and stir again. Return to microwave again for 1 to 2 minutes on high. (If this is too thick, add water for desired consistency.) Stir in margarine and vanilla. Put in pie shell; top with meringue. This is also good with whipped topping. (Refer to Meringue) Serves 6 to 8

Peaches and Cream Pie

½ cup powdered milk
½ cup sugar
Pinch of salt
¼ cup cornstarch
3 egg yolks
1½ to 2 cups water
1 teaspoon vanilla
2 to 3 tablespoons margarine
1 (16 ounce) can peach
    slices, drained and
    chopped
1 (9 inch) baked pie shell

Mix powdered milk, sugar and cornstarch; add egg yolks and water in microwave safe dish. Mix until smooth. Put in microwave for 2 minutes on high. Remove and stir well. Return to microwave for 2 more minutes on high. Remove and stir again. Return to microwave again for 1 to 2 minutes on high. (If this is too thick, add water for desired consistency.) Stir in margarine and vanilla. Cool to room temperature and fold in chopped peaches. Put in pie shell; top with whipped topping and garnish with reserved peach slices, if desired. Refrigerate. Serves 6 to 8

Rhubarb and Strawberry Pie

3 cups fresh rhubarb, sliced
3 cups fresh strawberries,
sliced
½ to ¾ cup sugar
1½ tablespoons instant
tapioca
⅓ cup fresh orange juice
1½ tablespoons orange
marmalade (optional)
¼ teaspoon orange peel
Pastry for double-crust pie
(9 inch)

Combine filling ingredients in large mixing bowl; let stand for 15 minutes while tapioca softens. Pour filling into pie shell. Prepare lattice strips for top crust. Bake at 400° for 20 minutes; reduce heat to 350° and bake 30 minutes more or until rhubarb is tender. This is always so good when spring comes and rhubarb and strawberries are in season. Serves 6 to 8

Very Berry Pie

1 cup sugar
Dash salt
¼ cup cornstarch
½ teaspoon cinnamon
1 cup blueberries
1 cup strawberries
¾ cup blackberries
¾ cup red raspberries
½ cup water
2 tablespoons lemon juice
2 tablespoons margarine
Pastry for a double-crusted
pie (9 inch)

In saucepan, combine sugar, salt, cornstarch, and cinnamon. Stir in berries. Add water and lemon juice. Cook over medium heat just to boiling point. Pour into pie shell; dot with margarine. Top with lattice or full crust, cut slits in top, brush with milk and sprinkle with sugar. Bake at 350° about 45 minutes or until crust is golden. This is delicious, top with ice cream for a special treat. Serves 8

God never keeps us at a post without assuring us of His presence, and sending us daily supplies.

Fruit and Nut Pie

4 apples, peeled and sliced
   (Granny Smith's are
   great)
1 cup cranberries
½ cup golden raisins
½ cup pecans or walnuts,
   chopped
1 cup sugar
⅔ cup brown sugar
4 tablespoons flour
1 teaspoon cinnamon
¼ teaspoon nutmeg
3 tablespoons margarine
Pastry for a double-crusted
   pie (9 inch)

Mix all ingredients together in large bowl. Pour into pie shell; cover with top crust. Bake at 350° for 40 to 50 minutes. Delicious for the holidays. Serves 8

Double Layer Pumpkin Pie

4 ounces cream cheese,
   softened
1 tablespoon milk
1 tablespoon sugar
1½ cups frozen whipped
   topping, thawed
1 graham cracker pie crust
1 cup milk
2 (3.4 ounce) packages
   vanilla flavored instant
   pudding and pie filling
1 (16 ounce) can pumpkin
1 teaspoon cinnamon
½ teaspoon ginger
¼ teaspoon cloves

Mix cream cheese, milk and sugar in large bowl until smooth. Gently stir in whipped topping. Spread on bottom of crust. Pour 1 cup milk into bowl. Add pudding mix. Beat until well blended, 1 to 2 minutes. (Mixture will be thick.) Stir in pumpkin and spices. Spread over cream cheese layer. Refrigerate at least 3 hours. Garnish with additional whipped topping and nuts, if desired. This is a great pie and a nice change from the plain pumpkin pie. Makes 8 servings

Success is not arriving at the summit of a mountain as final destination, but in continuing upwards.

Cranberry Pecan Pie

1 cup cranberries, fresh or
    frozen
3 eggs
1 cup brown sugar
¾ cup corn syrup (light or
    dark)
3 tablespoons margarine,
    melted
1 teaspoon vanilla
1 cup pecan halves
1 (9 inch) unbaked pie shell

In food processor or blender, grind berries coarsely. Set aside. In medium bowl, beat eggs with sugar. Stir in corn syrup, margarine and vanilla. Add pecans and cranberries. Pour into pie shell. Bake at 350° for 50 to 55 minutes or until knife inserted in center comes out clean. Cool and serve. The cranberries are a great mix with the pecans. Add a teaspoon of grated orange peel for a little extra zip. Serves 8

Apple Raisin Cream Pie

7 to 8 cups tart apples,
    peeled and sliced
1 cup sugar
½ cup flour
½ teaspoon nutmeg
1 teaspoon cinnamon
¾ cup raisins
Dash salt
1 to 2 teaspoons lemon rind,
    grated
1 tablespoon margarine
¾ cup heavy cream
Pastry for double-crust
    (10 inch) pie

Line bottom of pie pan with one crust and set aside. Combine apple slices, sugar, flour, spices, raisins, salt and lemon peel; mix together. Spoon filling into pastry-lined pan; dot with margarine. Cover with top crust decorated with steam vents. Seal edges. Cut a 1 inch circle in center of top crust. Bake at 350° for 40-45 minutes. Remove pie from oven; slowly pour cream into center hole of top crust. Return to oven; bake 5 to 10 minutes longer. Let stand 5 minutes before cutting. Refrigerate leftovers. This pie is so good, one of the treats we enjoy in the fall when apples come on. Serves 8 to 10

Sour Cream Lemon Pie

1 cup sugar
3½ tablespoons cornstarch
1 tablespoon lemon rind,
    grated
½ cup fresh lemon juice
3 egg yolks, slightly beaten
1 cup milk
¼ cup margarine
1 cup sour cream
1 (9 inch) baked pie shell
2 cups whipped topping,
    thawed
Lemon twists for garnish

Combine sugar, cornstarch, lemon rind, juice, egg yolks and milk in heavy saucepan; cook over medium heat until thick. Stir in margarine and cool mixture to room temperature. Stir in sour cream and pour filling into pie shell. Cover with whipped topping and garnish with lemon twists. Store in refrigerator. This is a wonderful pie and we like it in a graham cracker crust too. Serves 6 to 8

Frozen Chocolate Pie

1 (3 ounce) package cream
    cheese, softened
½ cup sugar
1 teaspoon vanilla
⅓ cup cocoa
⅓ cup milk
1 (8 ounce) carton frozen
    whipped topping, thawed
1 (9 inch) pie pastry, baked

In mixing bowl, beat cream cheese, sugar and vanilla until smooth. Add cocoa alternately with milk; mix well. Fold in whipped topping. Pour into pie shell. Freeze for 8 hours or overnight. Garnish with chocolate curls or chips. Serve directly from freezer. Serves 6 to 8

Ice Cream Delight

2½ cups cream-filled
   chocolate cookie crumbs,
   divided
½ cup margarine, melted
½ cup sugar
½ gallon chocolate, coffee
   or vanilla ice cream,
   softened
1½ cups salted peanuts
1 (8 ounce) carton frozen
   whipped topping, thawed

Chocolate Sauce:
2 cups powdered sugar
⅔ cup semisweet chocolate
   chips
1 (12 ounce) can evaporated
   milk
½ cup margarine
1 teaspoon vanilla

Combine 2 cups cookie crumbs with margarine and sugar. Press in bottom of 9 x 13 inch baking pan. Freeze for 15 minutes. Spread ice cream over crumbs; freeze until firm, about 3 hours. Combine first four sauce ingredients in saucepan; bring to boil. Boil for 8 minutes. Remove from heat and stir in vanilla; allow to cool to room temperature. Spoon sauce over ice cream; sprinkle with nuts. Freeze until firm. Spread whipped topping over nuts and sprinkle with remaining cookie crumbs. Freeze at least 3 hours before serving. Can be stored in freezer for up to a week. It is also delicious and makes a beautiful presentation when served. Serves 12-14

Cook's Tips

Whipping Cream
Real whipped cream is a special addition for many desserts. To whip cream, chill the bowl and beaters. Whip cream as close to serving time as convenient. Whip only until soft peaks form using care not to whip beyond this point. To sweeten whipped cream, add 1 to 2 tablespoons powdered sugar just before whipping is completed. The cornstarch in the powdered sugar helps to stabilize the whipped cream.

Pumpkin Cookies

½ cup shortening
1 cup sugar
1 cup pumpkin
2 cups flour
1 teaspoon baking powder
1 teaspoon soda
1 teaspoon cinnamon
½ teaspoon salt
1 teaspoon vanilla
¼ cup nuts
1 cup dates, chopped
   (optional)
1 cup raisins (optional)

Frosting
2 tablespoons margarine
1½ cups powdered sugar
Orange juice

Cream together shortening, sugar, and pumpkin. Add dry ingredients and mix well. Add nuts and dates/raisins. Drop by teaspoons on greased cookie sheet. Bake at 375° for 8 to 10 minutes. Remove from sheet immediately and cool on rack. Mix frosting ingredients, using orange juice to obtain desired consistency. Spread on cooled cookies. Excellent moist cookies. Makes 3 to 4 dozen

Oatmeal Cookies

1 cup shortening
1 cup sugar
1 cup brown sugar
2 eggs
1 teaspoon vanilla
1½ cups flour
1 teaspoon salt
1 teaspoon soda
3 cups oatmeal, can use
   quick or old fashioned
½ cup nuts, chopped

Mix sugars, shortening, eggs and vanilla. Add dry ingredients and nuts. Bake at 350° on lightly greased cookie sheet for 10 to 12 minutes or until golden brown. Take off cookie sheet immediately. Cool on a rack. Makes 3 to 4 dozen

Most people don't recognize opportunity because too many times it comes disguised as hard work.

Chocolate Chip Cookies

1½ cups shortening
¾ cup sugar
1½ cups brown sugar
1 teaspoon vanilla
3 large eggs
3½ cups flour
1½ teaspoons soda
1 teaspoon salt
2 cups chocolate chips
1 cup nuts, chopped
   (optional)

Mix shortening, sugar, brown sugar, vanilla and eggs together; beat until fluffy. Add dry ingredients and mix well. Add chocolate chips and nuts. Bake at 350° for 8 to 10 minutes or until golden brown. These are excellent cookies. Makes 5 to 6 dozen

Sugar Cookies

3 cups powdered sugar
2 cups margarine
2 eggs
1½ teaspoons vanilla
1 teaspoon almond flavoring
5 cups flour
2 teaspoons soda
2 teaspoons cream of tartar

Beat together powdered sugar, margarine, eggs and flavorings; add dry ingredients. Chill for 4 hours. Roll out on lightly floured board ¼ to ⅛ inch thickness. Cut with your favorite cookie cutters. Bake on ungreased cookie sheet at 350° for 10 to 12 minutes or until golden brown. Remove from cookie sheet and cool on rack. *These are excellent plain or frosted. This is a super recipe to use for decorated cookies. Frost with Butter Creme Frosting (refer to index) that has been colored to achieve your desired results. Kids and adults loves these cookies.* Makes several dozen

Double Treat Cookies

1 cup shortening
1 cup sugar
1 cup brown sugar
2 eggs
1 teaspoon vanilla
1 cup peanut butter
2 cups flour
2 teaspoons soda
½ teaspoon salt
1 cup salted peanuts,
    chopped
1 cup chocolate chips

Mix shortening, sugar, brown sugar, eggs, vanilla and peanut butter together. Add dry ingredients; mix well. Stir in chocolate chips and nuts. Shape into balls and flatten with a glass dipped in sugar. Bake at 350° for 10 to 12 minutes or until golden brown. These have always been my kid's favorite with the peanut butter and chocolate chips. Makes 3 to 4 dozen

Dad's Favorite Cookies

1 cup raisins
1 cup water
1 cup shortening
1 cup sugar
1 egg
6 tablespoons raisin juice,
    cooled
2 cups flour
1 teaspoon soda
1 teaspoon cinnamon
½ teaspoon nutmeg
¼ teaspoon cloves
½ teaspoon salt
2 cups oats, old fashioned
1½ cups chocolate chips

In saucepan add raisins and water. Bring to boil; cool. Meanwhile, mix sugar, shortening, and egg together. Add cooled raisin juice. Add dry ingredients. Mix in chocolate chips and drained raisins. Bake at 350° for 8 to 10 minutes or until golden brown. *This is our Dad's favorite cookie! It is an old family recipe that came from a great aunt. Also unusual with the cooked raisins - boy are they good!* Makes 3 to 4 dozen

Expect great things and great things will happen.

Chocolate Nut Chippers

¾ cup sugar
¾ cup brown sugar
¼ cup oil
1 teaspoon vanilla
1 egg
1 (5½ ounce) package
    chocolate fudge pudding
    and pie filling mix (not
    instant)
1 cup sour cream
2 cups flour
1½ cups oats
1 teaspoon soda
½ teaspoon salt
2 cups pecans, chopped
2 cups chocolate chips

Combine sugars, oil, vanilla, egg, pudding mix and sour cream. Mix at low speed until moistened. Add dry ingredients and mix until blended. By hand, stir in nuts and chocolate chips. Drop by rounded tablespoons on greased cookie sheet. Bake at 350° for 6 to 10 minutes or until set. Cool 1 minute before removing from cookie sheet. These are yummy, moist cookies. Makes 5 to 6 dozen

German Chocolate Cake Cookies

Frosting
1 cup sugar
1 cup evaporated milk
½ cup margarine, softened
1 teaspoon vanilla
3 egg yolks, beaten
1½ cups coconut
1½ cups pecans, chopped

Cake
1 German chocolate cake mix
⅓ cup margarine, melted

Mix frosting ingredients, except coconut and pecans; cook until thickened. Stir in coconut and pecans. Cool to room temperature. Reserve 1½ cups frosting. In large bowl, combine cake mix, margarine and remaining frosting, stir until moistened. Roll dough into balls and with your thumb, make indentation; add 1 teaspoon reserved frosting. Bake at 350° for 10 to 13 minutes. Cool 5 minutes and take off cookie sheet. Yummy cookies! Makes 4 to 5 dozen

Ginger Cookies

2 cups sugar
1½ cups margarine, softened
½ cup molasses
2 eggs
4½ cups flour
3 teaspoons baking soda
½ teaspoon salt
2 teaspoons cinnamon
1 teaspoon cloves
1 teaspoon ginger
½ teaspoon nutmeg
Sugar

In large bowl, beat sugar, margarine, molasses and eggs until light and fluffy. Add dry ingredients. Mix well. Cover with plastic wrap; refrigerate one hour. Shape dough into 1 inch balls, roll in sugar. Place 2 inches apart on ungreased cookie sheet. Bake at 350° for 8 to 12 minutes or until set. (Cookies will puff up and flatten during baking.) Cool 1 minute; remove from cookie sheet. *These cookies remind you of the ginger snaps you dunked in milk as a kid.* Makes 8 dozen

No-Bake Chocolate Cookies

2 cups sugar
½ cup milk
½ cup margarine
6 tablespoons cocoa
3 cups quick oats
½ cup nuts, chopped
1 teaspoon vanilla

Put sugar, margarine, cocoa and milk in saucepan and bring to boil, stirring constantly. Boil 3 to 4 minutes. Remove from heat and stir in oats, nuts and vanilla. Stir well. Drop by teaspoons full on waxed paper. *When we were kids, we loved going to Evelyn's house for these treats!* Makes 3 dozen

Submission to the divine will is the softest pillow on which to recline.

Peanut Blossoms

1¾ cups flour
½ cup sugar
½ cup brown sugar
1 teaspoon soda
½ teaspoon salt
½ cup shortening
½ cup peanut butter
1 egg
2 tablespoons milk
1 teaspoon vanilla
48 milk chocolate candy
    kisses

Combine all ingredients except candy kisses. Blend well at low speed. Shape into 1 inch balls. Roll balls in additional sugar. Place on ungreased cookie sheet. Bake at 375° for 10 to 12 minutes. Remove from oven. Top each cookie immediately with a candy kiss, pressing down firmly so cookie cracks around edges. *All kids, young and old, love these cookies with "kisses"!* Makes 3 to 4 dozen

Ginger Oatmeal Cookie

1 cup brown sugar
¾ cup margarine, softened
1 egg
¼ cup light molasses
1 teaspoon vanilla
1¾ cups flour
2 teaspoons baking soda
1 teaspoon cinnamon
½ teaspoon ginger
½ teaspoon cloves
2 cups quick oats
1 cup raisins (optional)
1 cup nuts, chopped
    (optional)

Beat brown sugar, margarine, egg, molasses and vanilla until well blended. Add dry ingredients and mix well. Drop by rounded tablespoons on greased cookie sheet. Bake at 350° for 7 to 12 minutes or until golden brown. Immediately remove from cookies sheet. These cookies can be kept in an airtight container for soft, moist cookies or leave container open for a more crisp cookie. Great, no matter what your preference. Makes 4 dozen

It is your business to learn to be peaceful and safe in God in every situation.

Cheesecake

Crust
⅓ cup powdered sugar
1½ cups graham cracker
    crumbs
½ cup margarine, melted

Filling
1 cup sugar
3 (8 ounce) packages cream
    cheese, softened
1½ teaspoons vanilla
4 eggs

Mix crust ingredients together and press in bottom of spring-form pan. Beat all filling ingredients together. Pour into crust. Bake at 350° for 50 to 60 minutes. Cool and remove sides of pan. Chill several hours before serving. This can be served with a fruit topping or plain. Excellent both ways. Serves 15 to 18

Chocolate Cake

2 eggs
1 cup cream
¾ cup milk
1 cup sugar
1 teaspoon vanilla
2 cups flour
1 teaspoon soda
½ teaspoon salt
3 tablespoons cocoa

Beat eggs, add cream, milk, sugar and vanilla and continue beating. Add dry ingredients and mix well. Grease and flour pans. Bake in 9 x 13 inch pan or two 8 inch layer pans at 325° for 30 to 35 minutes or until it springs back when you touch it. Excellent moist cake. If you omit the cocoa, this makes a super white cake. *My husband and son make this cake for the Cub Scout cake contest - a sure sign that it is easy!* Serves 12

Cake Servings For Two Layer Cakes
   6 inch serves 10
   8 inch serves 20
   9 inch serves 25
   10 inch serves 30 to 35
   12 inch serves 40 to 45
   14 inch serves 60 to 65
   16 inch serves 85 to 95
   18 inch serves 105 to 115

Chocolate Sheath Cake

½ cup margarine
½ cup shortening
4 tablespoons cocoa
1 cup cold water
2 cups flour
2 cups sugar
½ cup buttermilk
1 teaspoon cinnamon
½ teaspoon salt
1 teaspoon soda
2 eggs

Frosting
½ cup margarine
4 tablespoons cocoa
5 tablespoons milk
1 teaspoon vanilla
1 cup nuts, chopped
3½ cups powdered sugar

Bring to boil, margarine, short-ening, cocoa and water. Pour this mixture into bowl with flour and sugar. Mix well. Add all other ingredients. Pour into well greased 11 x 17 inch cookie sheet. Bake for 20 minutes at 400°. Five minutes before cake is done, bring to boil, margarine, cocoa and milk. Remove from heat; add vanilla, nuts and pow-dered sugar. Spread on cake when you take it from oven. Serves 24

Applesauce Cake

1 cup shortening
1¾ cups sugar
1 egg
3 cups applesauce
4 cups flour
2 teaspoons soda
1 teaspoon salt
1 teaspoon allspice
2 teaspoons cinnamon
1 teaspoon cloves
2 tablespoons hot water
1 cup raisins
1 cup walnuts, chopped

Cream shortening and sugar un-til fluffy. Add egg, applesauce, and water. Add dry ingredients. Stir in raisins and nuts. Pour into greased and floured 9 x 13 inch pan. (Can also bake in bundt or tube pan.) Bake at 350° for 1 hour or until it springs back when you touch it. Frost with desired frosting.

1 pound powdered sugar equals 3½ cups.

Mississippi Mud Cake

4 eggs
2 cups sugar
1 cup margarine
1½ cups flour
3 tablespoons cocoa
1½ cups coconut, flaked
1 cup nuts, chopped
1 teaspoon vanilla
1 large jar marshmallow
   creme

Frosting
½ cup margarine
3½ cups powdered sugar
⅓ cup cocoa
⅓ cup milk
1 teaspoon vanilla

Cream together eggs, sugar, margarine and vanilla. Add flour and cocoa; mix well. Add coconut and nuts. Place in a greased and floured 9 x 13 inch pan. Bake at 350° for 30 to 40 minutes. As soon as cake comes from oven, spread marshmallow creme over hot cake. Cool completely. Mix together frosting ingredients. Spread on cooled cake. Refrigerate. This is so rich and yummy! (There is no leavening in this cake.)

Oatmeal Cake

1 cup oatmeal, quick
1½ cups boiling water
½ cup margarine
1 cup brown sugar
1 cup sugar
2 eggs
1½ cups flour
1 teaspoon cinnamon
½ teaspoon nutmeg
1 teaspoon soda
½ teaspoon salt

Frosting
½ cup margarine
½ cup brown sugar
¼ cup cream
1 cup nuts, chopped
1 cup coconut
1 teaspoon vanilla

Mix oatmeal and boiling water together; let stand for 20 minutes. Beat margarine, sugars and eggs together. Add oatmeal mixture and dry ingredients; mix well. Bake at 350° in a 9 x 13 inch greased and floured pan for 35 to 40 minutes. In saucepan, bring margarine, sugar and cream to boil. Remove from heat; add nuts, coconut and vanilla. Spread on cooled cake. This cake is so moist and good.

Carrot Cake

2 cups sugar
1½ cups oil
4 eggs
2 cups carrots, grated
1 (8½ ounce) can pineapple,
    crushed and drained
2 cups flour
2 teaspoons baking powder
1½ teaspoons soda
1½ teaspoons salt
2 teaspoons cinnamon
1 cup coconut, flaked,
    (optional)
½ cup nuts, chopped
1 cup raisins (optional)
¾ cup chocolate chips

Frosting
½ cup margarine
4 cups powdered sugar
1 (8 ounce) package cream
    cheese, softened
1 teaspoon vanilla
Milk

Mix sugar, oil, eggs, carrots and pineapple together. Add dry ingredients. Add optional ingredients desired. Grease and flour 9 x 13 inch pan. Bake at 350° for 35 to 45 minutes or until the cake springs back when you touch it. Mix frosting ingredients, adding milk for desired spreading consistency. Spread on cooled cake.

Chocolate Chip Cake

1 cup margarine
1 cup sugar
2 eggs, beaten
1 teaspoon vanilla
1 teaspoon soda
½ teaspoon salt
2 tablespoons cocoa
1¾ cups flour
1 cup chocolate chips
1 cup boiling water
1 cup dates, chopped
¾ cup nuts, chopped

Pour boiling water over dates. Beat shortening and sugar. Add eggs and vanilla; mix well. Add dates and water alternately with dry ingredients. Sprinkle chips and nuts on top. Bake in a greased 9 x 13 inch pan at 350° for 30 to 45 minutes. The dates are a different twist with the chocolate, but really makes a moist cake.

Caramel Apple Cake

1¾ cups flour
1 cup brown sugar
½ teaspoon salt
½ teaspoon baking powder
½ teaspoon soda
1½ teaspoons cinnamon
1 teaspoon vanilla
¾ cup margarine, softened
3 eggs
1½ cups apples, peeled and
    chopped
1 cup nuts, chopped
½ cup raisins (optional)

Frosting
2 cups powdered sugar
¼ teaspoon cinnamon
¼ cup margarine, melted
½ teaspoon vanilla
4 to 5 teaspoons milk

In large bowl, combine flour, sugar, salt, baking powder, soda, cinnamon, vanilla, margarine and eggs. Mix on medium for 3 minutes. Stir in apples, nuts and raisins. Pour into greased and floured 9 x 13 inch pan. Bake at 350° for 30 to 40 minutes or until toothpick inserted in center comes out clean. Cool completely. In small bowl, blend all frosting ingredients, adding enough milk for desired spreading consistency. Spread over cooled cake. Serves 15

Chocolate Cherry Cake

1 package chocolate cake
    mix
1 (21 ounce) can cherry pie
    filling
1 teaspoon almond extract
2 eggs, beaten

Frosting
1 cup sugar
5 tablespoons margarine
⅓ cup milk
1 cup semi-sweet chocolate
    chips

In large bowl, combine all cake ingredients. By hand, stir until well mixed. Pour into a greased and floured 9 x 13 inch pan. Bake at 350° for 30 to 35 minutes or until toothpick inserted in center comes out clean. In saucepan, combine sugar, margarine and milk. Boil 1 minute, stirring constantly. Remove from heat; stir in chocolate chips until smooth. Pour and spread over warm cake. This cake can be baked in a bundt pan for a prettier presentation. Serves 12 to 16

Apple Pudding Cake
with Cinnamon Butter Sauce

Cake
1 cup brown sugar
¼ cup margarine, softened
1 egg
1 cup flour
1 teaspoon soda
1 teaspoon cinnamon
½ teaspoon nutmeg
¼ teaspoon salt
2 cups apples, chopped

Sauce
⅓ cup margarine
⅔ cup sugar
⅓ cup half-and-half
½ teaspoon cinnamon

In large bowl, beat brown sugar and margarine until light and fluffy; beat in egg. Add dry ingredients, mix well. Stir in apples. Spread batter in a greased 8 inch square pan. Bake at 350° for 25 to 30 minutes or until toothpick inserted in center comes out clean. Meanwhile, combine all sauce ingredients in small saucepan. Heat over medium heat until margarine melts and sauce is hot, stirring frequently. Serve warm sauce over warm cake. *This cake is almost like a pudding and really delicious with the sauce.* Serves 9

Pumpkin Cream Cheese Roll

1 cup sugar
3 eggs
⅔ cup pumpkin
¾ cup flour
1 teaspoon baking powder
2 teaspoons cinnamon
½ teaspoon nutmeg
½ teaspoon salt
1 cup nuts, chopped

Filling
1 cup powdered sugar
6 tablespoons margarine
**1 (8 ounce) package cream
    cheese, softened**
1 teaspoon vanilla

Mix sugar, eggs and pumpkin; add dry ingredients and nuts. Pour in greased and floured 11 x 17 inch cookie sheet. Bake at 375° for 15 minutes or until it springs back when touched. Remove from oven and turn upside down on a towel dusted with powdered sugar. Roll up in towel, like a jelly roll, starting with narrow end. Cool. Meanwhile, mix together filling ingredients. After roll is cooled, unroll and spread with filling. Roll up. Put on pretty serving platter, cut in one inch slices. This is such a good dessert and looks like you have spent hours fixing it.

Fruit Pizza

½ cup margarine
½ cup oil
1 cup sugar
1 egg
1 teaspoon vanilla
2½ cups flour
1 teaspoon salt
1 teaspoon soda
1 teaspoon cream of tartar

Filling
12 ounces cream cheese, softened
¾ cup powdered sugar
1½ teaspoons vanilla
Assorted fruits

Glaze
½ cup water
½ cup orange juice
2 tablespoons lemon juice
½ cup sugar
3 teaspoons cornstarch

Mix together margarine, oil, sugar, egg and vanilla. Add dry ingredients. Spread in 11 x 17 inch cookie sheet and bake at 300° for 20 to 25 minutes. Cool. Mix together filling ingredients and spread on cooled crust. Top with fruit of your choice (strawberries, blueberries, kiwi, grapes, peaches, etc.). Slice and arrange to make a pretty presentation. Mix sugar and cornstarch together in saucepan; add liquids. Cook over low heat stirring constantly until thickened. Cool glaze. Brush over top of fruit. This makes a beautiful dessert and is so refreshing. Serves 15 to 18

Eva's Fudge Bars

1 cup sugar
½ cup margarine
¼ cup milk
2 eggs
1 teaspoon vanilla
2 tablespoons cocoa
1 cup flour
½ cup nuts, chopped

Mix all together and spread in a 10 x 15 inch cookie sheet. Bake at 325° for 20 to 25 minutes. Frost with Pootsy's Chocolate Frosting. (refer to index) (There is no leavening in this recipe.) Serves 15

1 pound granulated sugar equals 2 cups.

Coffee Bars

2 cups brown sugar
2 eggs
⅔ cup oil
1 cup coffee, warmed
3 cups flour
1 teaspoon soda
1 teaspoon salt
2 cups chocolate chips
1 cup nuts, chopped

Mix everything except the chocolate chips and nuts. Pour into an 11 x 17 inch cookie sheet. Top with chocolate chips and nuts. Bake at 350° for 30 to 35 minutes. This is a quick and easy dessert and they are so good. Serves 15 to 18

Salted Peanut Bars

1½ cups flour
⅔ cup brown sugar
½ teaspoon salt
½ teaspoon baking powder
¼ teaspoon soda
½ cup margarine, softened
1 teaspoon vanilla
2 egg yolks
3 cups miniature
    marshmallows

Topping
⅔ cup corn syrup
¼ cup margarine
2 teaspoons vanilla
2 cups peanut butter chips
2 cups crisp rice cereal
2 cups peanuts

In large bowl, combine all ingredients, except marshmallows, until crumb mixture forms. Press in bottom of ungreased 9 x 13 inch pan. Bake at 350° for 12 to 15 minutes. Remove from oven. Immediately sprinkle with marshmallows. Return to oven for 1 to 2 minutes or until marshmallows just begin to puff. Cool while preparing topping. In saucepan, heat corn syrup, margarine, vanilla and peanut butter chips just until chips are melted and mixture is smooth, stirring constantly. Remove from heat; stir in cereal and nuts. Immediately spoon warm topping over marshmallows and spread to cover. Chill; cut into bars. *These are so yummy, you will think you are eating a candy bar.* Makes 36 bars

1 pound brown sugar equals 2½ cups.

Chocolate Marshmallow Bars

¾ cup margarine
1½ cups sugar
3 eggs
1 teaspoon vanilla
1⅓ cups flour
½ teaspoon baking powder
½ teaspoon salt
3 tablespoons cocoa
½ cup nuts, chopped
4 cups miniature
　marshmallows

Topping
1⅓ cups chocolate chips
3 tablespoons margarine
1 cup peanut butter
2 cups crisp rice cereal

In mixing bowl, mix margarine and sugar, add eggs and vanilla; beat until fluffy. Add dry ingredients. Stir in nuts. Spread in greased jelly roll pan. Bake at 350° for 15 to 18 minutes. Sprinkle marshmallows evenly over cake; return to oven for 2 to 3 minutes. Using a knife dipped in water, spread the melted marshmallows evenly over cake. Cool. For topping, combine chocolate chips, margarine and peanut butter in small saucepan. Cook over low heat, stirring constantly, until melted and well blended. Remove from heat; stir in cereal. Spread over bars. Chill. *Matt loves these for school treats!* Makes 3 dozen

Peanut Butter Swirl Bars

½ cup margarine
½ cup sugar
½ cup brown sugar
1 egg
½ cup peanut butter
½ teaspoon soda
¼ teaspoon salt
½ teaspoon vanilla
1 cup flour
1 cup oats, quick
2 cups chocolate chips

Frosting
½ cup powdered sugar
¼ cup peanut butter
4 tablespoons cream

Mix margarine, sugars, egg, peanut butter, and vanilla. Add dry ingredients except chocolate chips. Spread in 9 x 13 inch pan. Bake at 350° for 20 to 25 minutes. Remove from oven. Immediately sprinkle 2 cups chocolate chips on hot cake. Let stand 5 minutes; spread evenly over bars. Combine frosting ingredients. Drizzle and spread over chocolate. These are one of my kid's favorites! Serves 15

Caramel Pecan Bars

1 package yellow cake mix
¼ cup margarine
4 cups pecans, chopped or
   halves
1 cup brown sugar
½ cup sugar
1 cup margarine
½ cup honey
½ cup cream

Place cake mix in large bowl. Using pastry blender or fork, cut in ¼ cup margarine until mixture resembles coarse crumbs. Press in bottom of ungreased 10 x 15 inch cookie sheet. Top with pecans. In saucepan, combine brown sugar, sugar, 1 cup margarine and honey. Bring to a full boil over medium heat, stirring constantly. Boil three minutes; remove from heat. Stir in cream until well blended. Pour filling evenly over pecans. Bake at 350° for 17 to 22 minutes or until entire surface is bubbly. Cool completely; cut into squares or bars. Makes 48 bars

 1 pound shelled pecans or walnuts equals 4 cups.

Yogurt Apple Squares

2 cups flour
2 cups brown sugar
½ cup margarine, softened
1 cup nuts, chopped
2 teaspoons cinnamon
1 teaspoon soda
½ teaspoon salt
1 cup plain yogurt
1 egg
2 cups apples, peeled and
　　chopped

In large bowl, combine flour, sugar, and margarine; blend at low speed until crumbly. Stir in nuts. Press 2¾ cups of crumb mixture into ungreased 9 x 13 inch pan. To remaining mixture, add cinnamon, soda, salt, yogurt, vanilla and egg; blend well. Stir in apples. Spoon evenly over crust. Bake at 350° for 30 to 40 minutes or until toothpick inserted in center comes out clean. Cut into squares. Serve either plain or with whipped cream or ice cream. Excellent dessert. Serves 12

Danish Apple Bars

Crust
2½ cups flour
½ teaspoon baking powder
1 teaspoon salt
1 tablespoon sugar
1 cup shortening
½ teaspoon vanilla
1 egg, separated
Milk

Filling
1 cup cornflakes, crushed
4 to 5 apples, peeled and
　　sliced
1 cup sugar
1 teaspoon cinnamon

Glaze
1 cup powdered sugar
1 teaspoon hot water
½ teaspoon vanilla

Mix dry ingredients. Cut in shortening as for pie crust. Mix egg yolk, plus milk, to equal ⅔ cup liquid, add vanilla. Combine with dry ingredients. Divide dough in half. Roll out to fit a 12 x 15 inch pan. Over top of dough, sprinkle cornflakes and a layer of apples. Sprinkle with sugar and cinnamon. Roll out rest of dough and put on top, moisten edges and seal well. Beat egg white, brush on top. Bake at 400° for 10 minutes. Reduce heat to 350° and bake 35 to 40 minutes. Mix glaze ingredients. Drizzle over the top of warm bars. Excellent dessert. Makes 12 to 15

Brownies

4 squares unsweetened
   chocolate (or 8
   tablespoons cocoa)
⅔ cup shortening
2 cups sugar
4 eggs
1½ cups flour
1 teaspoon baking powder
1 teaspoon salt
1 cup nuts, chopped

Melt chocolate and shortening in microwave. Beat in sugar and eggs. Add dry ingredients and mix well. Stir in nuts. Spread in greased 9 x 13 inch pan. Bake at 350° for 30 to 35 minutes. If desired, spread with Pootsy's Chocolate Frosting before cutting. (refer to index) These brownies are moist and delicious. Makes 24 brownies

Maple Baked Apples

6 large baking apples
2 tablespoons lemon juice
½ cup raisins
½ teaspoon cinnamon
1 cup maple syrup
¼ cup water

Core apples and remove 1 inch strip of peel around top to prevent splitting. Brush tops and insides with lemon juice. Place apples in 1½ quart baking dish. In small bowl, combine raisins and cinnamon; fill center of each apple with mixture. Pour maple syrup over apples. Add ¼ cup water to baking dish. Bake at 350° for 45 to 50 minutes or until apples are tender, occasionally spooning syrup mixture over apples. *These are delicious!!* Serves 6

1 square chocolate can be substituted with 3 tablespoons cocoa.

Pootsy's Chocolate Frosting

1 tablespoon margarine,
    melted
1 square chocolate (or 2
    tablespoons cocoa)
1½ tablespoons warm water
1 cup powdered sugar

Mix all together until smooth.
Use on brownies, cakes or bars.

Chocolate Cream Cheese Frosting

1 (3 ounce) package cream
    cheese, softened
1 tablespoon milk
2½ cups powdered sugar
2 squares unsweetened
    chocolate, melted
1 teaspoon vanilla
Dash of salt

Blend cream cheese and milk.
Beat in powdered sugar and
chocolate; add vanilla and salt.
(Thin with more milk for desired
spreading consistency.) Will
frost a 9 x 13 inch cake.

Butter Creme Frosting

1¼ cups shortening
6 cups powdered sugar
1 teaspoon salt dissolved
    in ½ cup water
Flavoring to taste

Beat all ingredients until smooth
and fluffy. This is a great frosting
for coloring for sugar cookies.

Cherry Raspberry Sauce

1 (21 ounce) can cherry pie
    filling
1 (10 ounce) package frozen
    raspberries with syrup,
    thawed

In large bowl, gently combine pie
filling and raspberries. Serve
over ice cream or cake. Store
covered in refrigerator. Makes
3½ cups

Index

INDEX